WASHINGTON'S
CENTRAL CASCADES
FISHING GUIDE

NORTH BEND, SNOQUALMIE PASS,
ALPINE LAKES WILDERNESS & CLE ELUM

BY DAVE SHORETT

Acknowledgements

I wish to thank the following persons for their time and help in making this book possible: Eric Anderson, Chris Axling, Jim Cummins, Bill Dowdy, Mark Downan, Jennifer Evans, Curt Kraemer, Ted Lloyd, Tyler Patterson, Peter Shorett, and Phil White.

Copyright 2001

ISBN 0-9652116-2-2

Publisher: LakeStream Publications. 200 Maynard Building, 119 1st Avenue South, Seattle, WA 98104-2533. Phone: (206) 842-9202.

Photo credits

All photos in this book are the author's except:
USFS photos on pages 17, 43, 44, 51, 52, 53, 55, 56, 57 ,61, 75, 78, 79, 80, 82
Chris Axling photos on pages 68, 69, and back cover photo.

Maps

Graymouse Graphics, 2826 11th Ave E. Seattle, Wa. 98102   206-325-7543.

Design

Martha Brouwer, Loft Publishing, Seattle, WA 98117 206-781-3347.

Warning

Hiking and fishing are potentially hazardous. Anglers and hikers must assume responsibility for their actions and safety. This book is merely a guidebook and cannot and does not disclose all risks, potential or otherwise, which exist in the activities and geographic areas it describes. Good topographical maps, compass, and common sense are essential to hiking and fishing in the Central Cascades. USFS Rangers can answer questions about weather, road conditions, trail status, animal and other hazards, access, cross-country travel, and a host of other matters. Always consult with them to get up-to-date information.

CONTENTS

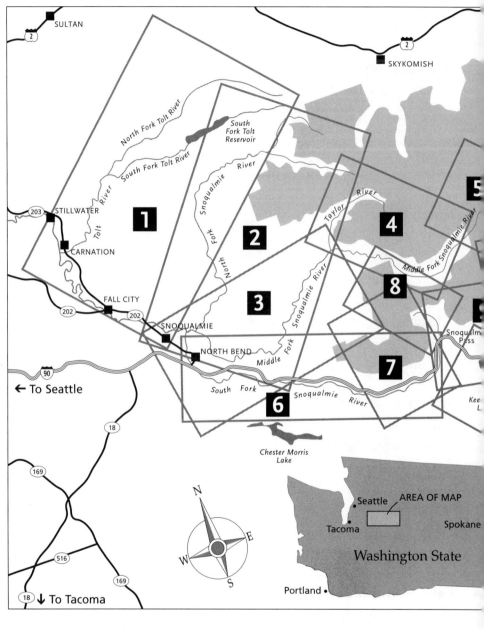

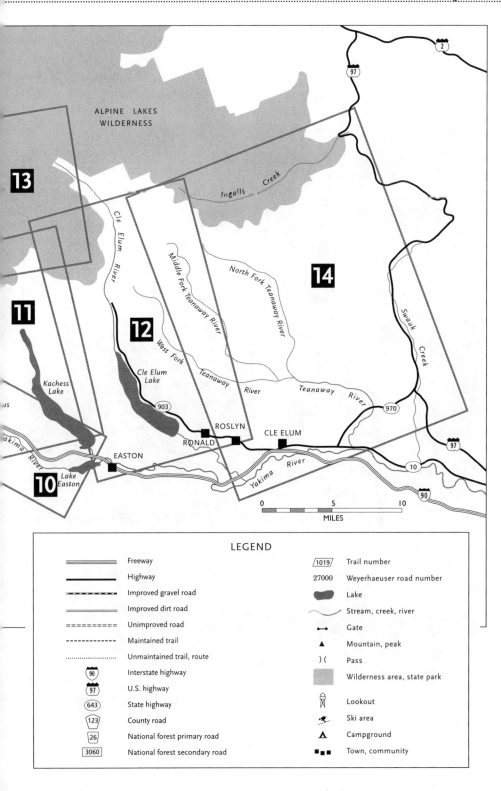

ALPINE LAKES
WILDERNESS

13

11

12

14

Ingalls Creek

Cle Elum River

Middle Fork Teanaway River

North Fork Teanaway River

Swauk Creek

West Fork

Kachess
Lake

Cle Elum
Lake

Teanaway

River

Teanaway   River

903

970

Yakima River

EASTON

RONALD

ROSLYN

CLE ELUM

Lake
Easton

10

Yakima   River

97

2

97

10

90

0   5   10

MILES

LEGEND

═══════	Freeway	1019	Trail number
───────	Highway	27000	Weyerhaeuser road number
▬·▬·▬·▬	Improved gravel road	◖◗	Lake
═══════	Improved dirt road	∿	Stream, creek, river
==========	Unimproved road	⊶	Gate
─ ─ ─ ─ ─	Maintained trail	▲	Mountain, peak
············	Unmaintained trail, route	) (	Pass
90	Interstate highway	▓	Wilderness area, state park
97	U.S. highway		
643	State highway	⌂	Lookout
123	County road	⚶	Ski area
26	National forest primary road	▲	Campground
3060	National forest secondary road	■▪▪	Town, community

Flyfishing the Lower North Fork Snoqualmie River

INTRODUCTION

South Fork Snoqualmie Rainbow Trout

A s I drove up Edgewick Road out of North Bend, I began to glimpse the Middle Fork Snoqualmie River. It was a sunny, warm day in late August. The contrast between the city which I had left only 45 minutes ago and the forest, river, and mountain peaks which gradually came into view reminded me of how fortunate I am to live in the Puget Sound area. The glorious Middle Fork valley, with its fine river, several tributaries, many trails to scenic lakes with opportunities for great high lake fishing and cross-country access to other more remote lakes, is just one of many grand places to fish in Washington's Central Cascades.

I hiked to a small lake, fished it, hiked back and fished the Middle Fork before returning to the city. It took me a couple of hours to reach the lake, traveling up an old gated road then a steep trail. Fortunately, it was a calm day, fish were rising and I found a good place to stand on a bouldered point, where I could cast to them. My first cast, using a 14' leader with a size 14 parachute Adams, settled on the water gently, as I had hoped. I waited, completely focused on the fly, ignoring the beauty of the lake. Soon, a fat 11" rainbow grabbed the fly with a lunge. The next two were more difficult, as the first trout spooked the dead-

Angler Casting to Rising Trout on Central Cascades Lake

still lake for a time. I paused to eat my lunch and take in the scenery, then caught another fat rainbow.

As afternoon came on, I headed back down the trail to my car, drove downstream along the Middle Fork, looking for good spots to fish the rest of the day. The river was low and about as clear as it gets. There were insects in the air but there were no fish rising, not surprising since one rarely sees fish rise in the Middle Fork. I stopped next to a small reach with plenty of boulders, riffles and pockets, drove about a half mile farther down and parked off to the side.

I put on my waders, rigged up my rod again, with a size 12 Elk Hair Caddis and headed straight on through the trees and undergrowth toward the sound of the river. After the usual encounters with devils club, brush and leader grabbing bushes, I came out next to the river. It looked good upstream.

I telescoped out the wading staff I use on the Middle Fork, stepped gingerly into casting position, worked out some line and cast straight upstream, landing the Elk Hair close behind a boulder. Drag took the fly too fast downstream but I could see a small trout rush and miss it as it shot by. It was going to be a good day on the Middle Fork.

There are 25 streams and at least 210 lakes in the Central Cascades in the North Bend, Snoqualmie Pass, Cle Elum Area containing trout. You can fish in the company of others or in complete solitude; step out of the car and cast to trout in streams and lakes within minutes; bushwhack half an hour and fish a spot in a stream that is seldom visited; hike an hour or two to a mountain lake with abundant trout, some to good size, or to a remote stretch of stream; pack in for a weekend or for weeks to remote lakes and a few streams that go unfished most of the season; bushwhack cross-country to very isolated alpine areas in search of trout. In short, the Central Cascades have about every type of fishing one could hope for in a mountain area.

There is one limiting factor. If you are are after "trophy" trout in the Central Cascades, you'll have to fish the lakes to find one. The streams simply do not support large trout in any number. Any trout 16" or larger is extremely rare in Central Cascades rivers and creeks. Typically, most stream trout are in the 6-10" size class, with some to 12" and a few to about 15". Selective fishery regulations, defined as no bait, barbless single hook, seem to be resulting in a slow increase in numbers and size and there are positive signs, but anyone who claims to be catching even 15" fish with any regularity needs to be put under oath before telling you about his fishing. Not so for the lakes however, as knowledgeable anglers can find trout to 5 lbs. here and there and 16-18" trout are not rare in the area's high lakes.

There is good news in Central Cascades trout fishing. Many logging practices which damaged streams and lakes have been curtailed. Selective fishery regulations have increased trout populations. Limit your catch and catch and release ethics are now the rule, not the exception, and this has had a major impact on Central Cascades fishing. Most anglers also now practice the no-trace ethic and there is less environmental damage to the waters. Finally, fish stocking policies are now science-based and have substantially improved quality fishing in the high lakes. Sprawl and population growth in Puget Sound have not helped and will cause ever increasing pressure on the area, but if you are willing to walk a bit, hike some, or bushwhack, you will find plenty of great fishing for mountain trout in the Central Cascades.

How to Get There
Access to Central Cascades Lakes and Streams

This book is designed to give anglers the information they need to get to the streams and lakes of the Central Cascades, using the shortest distances whenever possible. Roads and trails are described as of the time of publication. The text is oriented from west to east, given the fact that most anglers will be traveling from the Puget Sound area.

Roads The Forest Service has at one time or another established a number for each of its roads. Most of its roads have numbers posted on signs, generally junction points. However, signs are sometimes missing, due to a variety of causes. Additionally, the Forest Service seems bent upon changing its numbering system from time to time. Up to date information and maps are usually available at Ranger Stations. Weyerhauser Co. has its own numbering system and it is also subject to change. If traveling on Weyerhauser property, a Weyerhauser map is necessary to find your way around.

Trails Many trails are numbered but some are not and trail signs are sometimes nonexistent or missing. Trail numbers are sometimes changed as well. Ranger Stations have both maps and current information.

Maps The maps in this book are meant to be only reference and starting points to plan your trip. They are set up in an overlapping fashion, so some of the same information will be contained on two or even three maps.

DO NOT USE THE MAPS IN THIS BOOK AS SUBSTITUTES FOR GOOD TOPOGRAPHIC MAPS. DO NOT ATTEMPT TO HIKE CROSS-COUNTRY WITHOUT A COMPASS AND A GOOD TOPOGRAPHIC MAP. A list of suitable topographic maps is found in the Appendix.

Central Cascades Streams

There are numerous rivers and creeks in the Central Cascades containing trout in fair to abundant numbers. All of the streams described in this book are within two hours driving time from Seattle, many within an hour or less.

Stream Management Policies

Before humans began stocking Central Cascades streams, the only trout known to exist in any Central Cascades streams were coastal cutthroat and rainbow on the West side and west slope cutthroat and rainbow on the East side. Bull trout, actually a char, and mountain whitefish were also native to many of these streams. (They may in fact, may be the only "genuine" native fish in most of these streams. There is no evidence of any introduction of bull trout or whitefish, yet they certainly reside in many rivers and a few creeks.)

Middle Fork Snoqualmie River

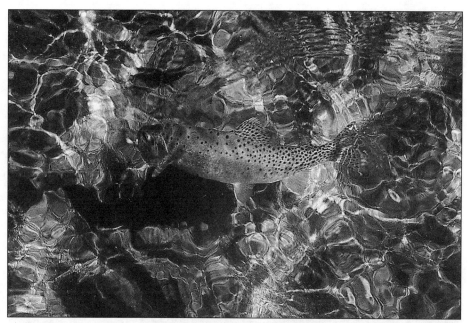

Teanaway River Cutthroat

For many years, the area's mountain streams were regularly planted with both west slope (Rocky Mountain) and coastal cutthroat, rainbow, sometimes eastern brook, and even grayling (which apparently never survived). Experimental planting occurred and streams which had native populations as well as those with no trout were planted. There was also an annual "put and take" trout fishery in many streams, involving stocking legal size trout on a regular basis. Bait fishing, especially salmon egg fishing, was the predominant technique.

In 1986, after a major study and public process, WDFW adopted a new stream management strategy intended to improve trout fishing on nearly 80 streams in the State. Many of those streams are in the Central Cascades. The streams affected by the plan now have a late May or June 1 opener to allow adult trout to spawn, a minimum length, usually 8 or 10," to allow females to spawn at least once before being retained by an angler, and bait prohibitions to enhance survival of released fish. Presently, the State stocks trout in few streams statewide and none of the streams in this guidebook. Evaluations made since the policy change have led to additions of other streams to this management scheme, catch and release regulations in some and other changes as well. Most streams are now under "selective fishing" regulations, which allow only flies or lures with one barbless hook.

The results are becoming noticeable in most such streams, though a few seem unaffected. All of the streams described in this guidebook now have self-sustaining, wild trout populations. Informal surveys suggest that fish in streams with selective fishing are slowly returning to a natural equilibrium with their environment, in numbers, sizes and ages. It is the author's view that this has meant generally at least

Flyfishing the Waptus River

a slight gradual increase in size and numbers of trout, especially where environmental conditions are not substantially affected by logging, road building, washouts, or other detrimental man-made factors.

Thus, the trout you catch in Central Cascades streams have never been in a hatchery and are wild fish. It is well to respect this and treat them accordingly, practicing catch and release even where it isn't required, unless regulations allow and you feel that keeping one or two to eat is appropriate.

Flyfishing Central Cascade Streams

With the exception of the Yakima River, Washington's blue ribbon trout stream, open to catch and release fishing all year, the following covers virtually all the streams in this guidebook.

When to Fish

Washington State Fishing Regulations set the seasons. A few streams are open year around, but generally streams open June 1 and close October 31.

Before runoff there is sometimes an early opportunity to fish some of the streams, particularly the small creeks. Nymph or spin fishing are generally necessary to have much action. However, runoff is often in full swing by June 1 and there is little fishing to be had until the streams settle down.

Early July offers the earliest decent fishing opportunity for most streams, with a few exceptions, such as the Teanaway system and sometimes the upper Tolt forks and the South Fork Snoqualmie, which can be good in a dry June. Most creeks are fishable by early July. After the rare very dry winter in Washington, many streams are fishable by late June.

Mid to late July is the time when most stream anglers begin fishing the major Central Cascades streams. They are beginning to warm, insects are moving and fish are feeding.

August is the month when the streams are in their best shape, the waters warm, insects hatch in good numbers, and fish are readily taken with dry flies.

Early to mid-September provides the best fishing on most area streams, with most waters at their lowest levels; trout are accessible and feed avidly. Dry fly fishing continues to be very good.

Late September often allows very good fishing, unless heavy rains hit or it becomes unseasonably cold. Trout become more sporadic in feeding at times, though.

Early October often has warm days along with its colder nights in the mountains, and trout begin to move to deeper pools and become less active, except during the warmth of the day.

Mid to late October are challenging times. Temperature, rain and a general hunkering down by trout make fishing tough but sometimes rewarding.

Five Stream Fishing Tips

1. Fish upstream whenever possible. The trout don't see you coming and you can read the water better.
2. Wading will improve your success, letting you get to more holding water.
3. Fishing "blind" is ok. This is not New Zealand – you will rarely be able to see a trout in these mostly fast moving waters and there are generally plenty of trout, though small, in the usual likely places. Cast your fly in those places as you work upstream.
4. Dry fly fishing is generally more effective than nymph, wet fly or streamer fishing.
5. Don't unnecessarily ford rivers. It rarely results in any better fishing, because spots which require fording will seldom hold fish larger than the ones you will catch in riffles, pockets and other likely spots reachable from a safe position. The "big one" is seldom on the other side of the river.

Equipment

Rods, reels, fly lines should be light, 2-5 weight ideally. Few of the fish you catch will be larger than 12." A 9' rod allows a lot of dapping on small rivers and creeks and is better, in the author's view, than a 7' rod, which is preferred by many.

Leaders for dry fly fishing should be as long as you can manage on streams. A long leader allows a fly to float drag-free longer, and keeps the fly line away from the fish. A 10-14' leader is best for rivers, slightly shorter ones function better on creeks. Nymph leaders can be much shorter, 5-7' depending upon how the nymph is fished. When using a dropper system, a leader 1.5 times the depth should extend below the indicator or floating fly. For children and beginners, the shorter the leader, the easier it is for them to cast.

Tippets for dry fly fishing should be 5x or 6x, 4x for nymphing.

Floatant is essential. You will rue the day you forget or lose your floatant because these streams are fast and riffly and you will need floatant constantly.

Waders are necessary to fish effectively in nearly all the rivers and larger creeks. Featherlight, nylon felt-sole bootfoot chest waders are preferred during most of the summer, with full neoprene waders necessary early and late in the season when the water temperature is quite cold. Hip boots will inevitably leave you wishing you had chest waders, except on small streams.

Stream Flies

The Big Three Dry Flies are about all that you need: Adams 12-16, Wulf, Royal, Grey, or Brown, 12-14, Elk Hair Caddis, 12-16. There are some anglers who use the Elk Hair Caddis nearly all the time.

Matching the hatch is rarely necessary. Central Cascades trout live in a fast-moving habitat and have to feed when the opportunity comes along. There are seldom significant hatches and even the occasional hatch is usually easily matched with one of the big three.

Nymphs, wet flies and streamers are very effective and can work when dry flies do not. Fish them weighted because they have little time to get down before being swept away, except in the infrequent slow-moving pool. Hare's Ear, Zug Bugs, and Caddis are the best along with your favorite soft hackle flies but anything that gets down well may work. Weighted small Wooly Buggers and Muddler Minnows all catch fish but are not nearly the fun that dry flies are.

Size 12 and 14, sometimes 16 are generally best for dry flies and a variety of sizes work for subsurface angling. If you are hooking steelhead and salmon smolts, go to a size 10 or even 8 to keep them off. Often, the largest trout will take a well-presented size 10 dry fly or terrestrial in these streams.

Central Cascades Lakes

Part of the excitement of fishing mountain lakes is the anticipation that comes with planning a trip, whether a day trip or weeks of hiking and fishing in the Cascades. The maps come out, the gear gets checked, maybe some new flies and lures are bought. The anticipation inevitably focuses on what kind of trout will there be, what size and how many.

Will there be fish in the lake? What species and what size?

This book attempts to tell the angler what is known historically and presently (2001) about each lake described. Accuracy is intended but not guaranteed. Many variables affect trout populations in these lakes.

S elf-sustaining trout populations now exlst In a surprising number of high lakes. Virtually none of the high lakes contained trout before they were introduced by early management practices, but once planted, many trout populations were able to reproduce and become self- sustaining. (Where there's a will there's a way) Some of these lakes have large numbers of reproducing trout; others a moderate number; a handful have very few; and others have only intermittent years when conditions are sufficient for spawning, occasionally with intervals so lengthy in a few that trout die out entirely.

Flyfishing a Central Cascades high lake.

Some species are more successful in becoming self-sustaining than others. Cutthroat generally do better in high lakes than rainbow, probably because of their spawning habits. Westslope cutthroat readily beach spawn, making them more successful than coastal cutthroat. Rainbow/cutthroat hybridization occurs sometimes, and there are reports of golden/rainbow hybridization. Golden trout are taxonomically rainbow trout, but only reproduce successfully in select coldwater situations. Eastern brook nearly always succeed in becoming self-sustaining, often to the extent of over-reproducing, resulting in stunted populations. Cutthroat can also occasionally over-produce and stunt, but much less often.

The book has attempted to state which lakes have self-sustaining populations. You should strongly consider catch and release in these lakes to allow their trout populations to continue to exist. There are some exceptions, notably eastern brook lakes, because with only the rare exception, a brookie population can only be made healthier by some harvest. Also, a few self-sustaining cutthroat lakes have small, stunted fish. Both types of such lakes are characterized by nearly all their fish being skinny trout with large heads, a sure sign of overproduction. In brookie lakes, you should feel free to take and eat your limit. (Brookies are said by many to be the best tasting trout to come out of a frying pan.) Rainbow rarely overpopulate a high lake. There is always an exception, even to an exception; some lakes have only a few stunted trout because the lake simply doesn't have a sufficient food supply to support more than a few trout of even small size. In such a lake, catch and release is necessary – you don't want to take the last trout, leaving the lake barren.

Management and Stocking policies change from time to time. Policy is developed by WDFW in conjunction with the Forest Service for lakes and streams on USFS land, and with the Washington Department of Natural Resources on DNR land. There is presently an increasing trend in lake management toward maintaining native species, limiting introduced species and even considering eradication of introduced species. Rainbow and coastal cutthroat are native to the region west of Snoqualmie Pass and in all probability will continue to be stocked. Golden trout are increasingly stocked because they are taxanomically the same as rainbow. Brook trout and brown trout are not native to Washington and it is likely that neither will be stocked in these lakes and removal may be considered. (In Mt. Rainier National Park, there have been attempts, some successful, to eradicate brookies from lakes.) West slope cutthroat are also not native to the west side of Snoqualmie Pass and it is likely they will be excluded from stocking there. They are native to the east side and will be part of the stocking program on the area east of the Pass.

Stocking policies are part of overall high lake management programs, which vary from time to time. At one time, it was believed that the more fry planted in a lake, the more trout, larger trout and better fishing there would be. Several high lake studies revealed though that each lake had its own ecology, optimal numbers and sizes of trout depended upon, simply stated, the food supply in each lake. Biologists studied nearly all of the high lakes and determined what would be the appropriate species, number, and interval for stocking each lake which required stocking to provide these optimal numbers, including lakes which had naturally reproducing populations resulting from earlier stocking. Many lakes with self-sustaining populations were then no longer stocked, some were supplemented with occasional or regular stocking. In general, a lot less trout were planted in most lakes, and the result has been healthy populations in the vast majority of lakes, with some lakes producing quite large trout. It is the author's view that current WDFW high lake management is very good and the resource is in good shape.

Actual stocking is done by WDFW and volunteer organizations under its direction. Unauthorized stocking is illegal in any Washington waters. WDFW employees do some of the actual delivery of fry to the high lakes, but volunteers from fishing clubs, most notably the Trailblazers, do a large percentage. (If you really want to become involved with what's going on with the high lakes in Washington, join the High Lakers and Trailblazers) Lakes don't always get stocked on schedule but WDFW has generally reliable stocking statistics.   The author has however found a number of times that a different species from the one reported by WDFW has been stocked.

Crystal Lake and Upper Tuscohatchie Lake

Stocking cycles affect trout sizes you will find in a given lake. If a lake is self-sustaining, you will generally find trout of all ages, from fry to older adult fish, some as old as 10 years and even older in rare cases. This will similarly be the case for self-sustaining lakes which are supplemented by stocking, except that the supplemented age group will have higher numbers. Depending upon spawning conditions, predation, weather, over-winter conditions, and cyclical food supply, the number of trout in each age group may vary significantly.

Lakes which are not self-sustaining and are stocked at regular intervals, as most stocked lakes are, will probably have trout of only two ages, those from the last stocking and those from the current stocking. If such a lake is stocked only occasionally, or erratically due to a number of factors, it may only have fish of one age group. If a lake is stocked every year, as a few high lakes are, it will have trout of all ages.

Thus, when you fish a high lake, if it has fish of all ages, it is very likely that it has natural reproduction. If there is only one size or two, it is likely that it depends upon stocking to contain trout.

Flyfishing Central Cascades High Lakes
Equipment

Rod, reel, fly line, and leader. A 9-foot two piece 4-5 weight rod in an aluminum case, which makes a decent walking staff if padded on both ends, or a similar 4 piece pack rod will do fine, and will work as a spinning rod if you want to spin fish. Any 4-5 weight graphite reel with two extra spools will work. You should have a 4-5 weight floating line, sink tip and full sinking line on the reel and extra spools. Leaders should be 10-14' if you can manage, shorter for children and beginners, but you can shorten up to 3-4' when fishing deep.

Rafts, float tubes or featherlight waders all will help you get your fly or lure out into the lake. It all depends upon your tolerance for carrying weight.

Ten High Lake Flies

1. Parachute Adams - 12-20.
2. Grey or Royal Wulf - 14-20.
3. Scud - 8-20 in a variety of colors.
4. Callibaetis Nymph - 14-18.
5. Chironomid Nymph - 10-18, in a variety of colors, red, brown, black, tan and olive.
6. Hare's Ear - 10-18.
7. Midge, Griffith's Gnat - 16-22 in black and gray.
8. Pheasant Tail Nymph - 14-18.
9. Wooly Bugger - 2-8 in black, tan, olive and brown.
10. Ant - 10-14.

Soft Hackles in a variety of colors and sizes are useful all-purpose flies and will often work with a variety of retrieves.

Five Best Places to Fish on a High Lake

Points usually allow casting room and have deeper water on one side or both sides.

Inlets where you can fish the edges of the flow into the lake. However, don't fish the inlet stream itself, as you may disturb spawning trout.

Logs extending into the lake are often the only place you can effectively cast a line. Be careful, for most of these logs are very slippery and some will sink under your weight.

Open shoreline where you have a clear path for backcasting and can get your fly or lure out into the lake.

Wind can make casting easier or more difficult. Try fishing with the wind at your back but be aware that heavy winds can push insects to the windward shore and that's where the trout may be concentrated, unless there are insects being blown off the trees into the near-shore water.

Spin Fishing

Spin fishing, when certain practices are followed, is very much a low-impact and effective way to fish Central Cascades streams and lakes. Double and triple hook lures are believed to be too hard on fish and cause an unacceptable mortality rate. There is also a tendency in spin fishing to horse a fish out of the water, including reeling them right up to the rod tip and dangling them. The use of reasonable drag and care of fish is essential.

Spin fishing can be particularly effective in streams when they are running full and are cloudy. It is fair to say that spin fishing is generally more effective in lakes than fly fishing if the angler knows how to use both hardware and flies. Many lakes are much more easily fished by spin casting than fly rod casting, particularly those with steep or heavily vegetated shorelines or shallow bottoms extending far out from shore, and there is no doubt that spin casting can get your lure or fly farther out into a lake.

Five High Lakes Fishing Tips

1. Raft and float tube fishing will greatly improve your success since you can fish the entire lake. It is generally necessary to fish with a lot of line out, as mountain trout are easily disturbed by what must look like a flying saucer crossing the lake.

2. Fish quietly, for high lakes are usually very still places and a lot of false casting, thrashing the water and noise will frighten these trout. Falling in is a major no-no.

3. Be Patient, especially when dry fly fishing. Even when fish are not rising, they are cruising, looking for food. When it is calm but there is no sign of feeding, you can still cast a good dry fly, such as an Adams or an ant, out into the lake, tighten your leader and relax, taking in the scenery but keeping an eye on your fly. That rise and take could occur any time.

4. Mornings and evenings are the best times to fish during the heat of the summer. Midday is often better during early and late season, because these lakes warm as the day goes on during early summer and fall days, cooling substantially at night.

5. Dropper fishing can be an effective technique, with a nymph hanging down a foot to several feet off the bend of a dry fly.

Ultralight or light spinning reels and rods are sufficient for Cascades trout. Four pound test line is plenty strong. To effectively fish flies with spinning gear, the spin angler shoud have a few casting bubbles, the dry flies, wet flies and nymphs recommended in this book, some split shot in a variety of sizes, and some fly floatant for bubble and dry fly fishing.

There is a vast arrary of lures availabe. A few suggestions, particularly for lakes, are single hook flatfish and triple teasers, dick nite, brass spoons for brookie lakes and small canadian wonderspoons, all of which come with single hooks. Others, which generally have to be converted from triple or double to single hook lures are roostertails, mepps and daredevils.

Spinners work better in streams and spoons are more effective in lakes. Across, down and back fishing is usually most effective in streams and getting near the bottom is important. Varying retrieves is helpful in lakes.

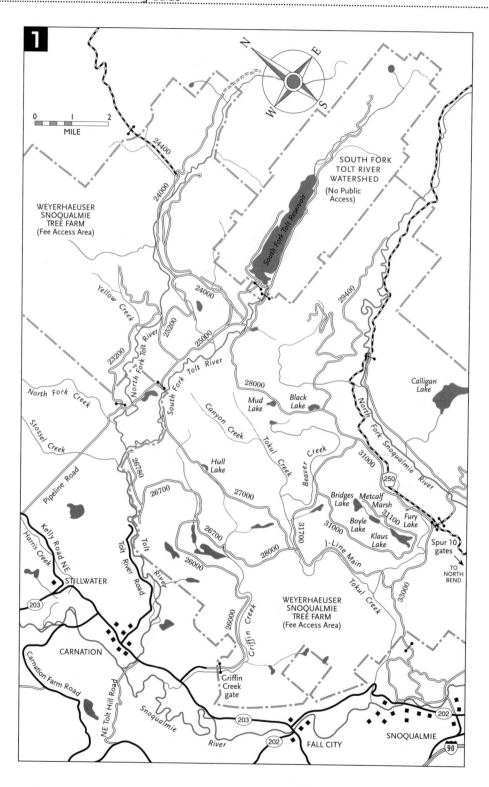

NORTH BEND

Upper Mainstem Tolt River

Mainstem Tolt River   (Map 1, 2)

The mainstem Tolt is well-known as a steelhead river but its upper reach below the junction of its forks provides good fishing at times for small trout, with a few to 12-13." There are not a lot of trout but most good lies will have a few fish. Use large flies to avoid Steelhead smolts. Access is difficult, as Weyerhauser has sold off much of its land along this part of the Tolt and there is now private ownership and development. The Carnation/Stillwater area is the starting point for finding a way to the upper mainstem Tolt. Steep banks border the river for the most part and a good deal of bushwhacking may be necessary to get to it, depending upon where one chooses to try to creep, crawl, slide, or maybe fall on the way down. Because the bordering land is in such a state of flux, no particular access route is recommended. One must search for a way to get to the Tolt but once there, a sunny day in mid to late summer on the river can recharge an angler's soul. The river is closed upstream from the USGS trolley cable near the confluence of the North and South Forks.

The North and South Forks of the Tolt are accessible from Weyerhauser land, by fee access permit only. The closest Weyerhauser access to the Tolt and its forks is through the Griffin Creek Gate off Highway 203. There are closed waters from the trolley cable to the mouth of Yellow Creek on the North Fork, and to the dam on the South Fork. The North Fork comes into shape somewhat earlier than most westside streams, as there is less melt flowing into the river than in many westside streams. It provides nice fishing for small trout in a remote area.

Mainstem Snoqualmie River

Anglers who know where, when and how to fish this 4 mile section of the river upstream from Snoqualmie Falls to the South, North and Middle Fork junctures find good fishing at times for predominately cutthroat and some rainbow, with the cutthroat occasionally to 15-18." In the early summer, the river is usually too high to fish, but by mid to late August it drops and clears. Access is difficult and wading is hazardous in most sections. The most effective fishing is from a boat. (Be sure to take out before you go over Snoqualmie Falls.) The river is for the most part broad and slow with few riffles, mainly long slow glides. There are lots of fry and small fish in this section of the Snoqualmie but 12-15" and larger cutthroat have historically been taken here.

High banks and deep water make flyfishing very tough in most of the mainstem above the falls. Those who can reach the area below the mouth of the South Fork can find good fishing late in the summer. Until then, this section of the river is generally too high for any dry fly fishing but spin fishing or fast sinking wet fly and streamer fishing can be effective. Spinning gear works best until hatches show up. Midday hatches are rare but evening hatches occur beginning in late July and continue through early September. Most trout are small but this short section of the Snoqualmie river does hold the largest trout in the Snoqualmie system.

Mt. Si Lakes

On the back side of Mt. Si are two 5 acre lakes at about 3400'. There is no trail and they are both very difficult to find. A long way from the nearest gate on a logging road, they require a walk of 6 miles on the old logging road then bushwhacking, often wet. Shallow **Crater lake** (3400) drains to the North Fork Snoqualmie River. It appears to have limited natural reproduction by rainbow, and may occasionally be supplemented by stocking. Catch and release should be practiced here. Much deeper **Rachor Lake** (3500) depends upon periodic stocking for its rainbow trout population.

Dayhiking to Central Cascades streams brings fast action

Rattlesnake Lake

This lake is the local fishing hole for North Bend residents. It is about half a mile from Cedar Falls, south of North Bend, via the 436th SE exit off I-90. Highly variable springs cause the lake to fluctuate greatly in volume and surface area through the summer months, varying between 50 and 100 acres. The lake is managed for selective regulation fishing for rainbow, with frequent plants keeping the action going through much of the summer. Drought years can bring changes in management and stocking but in years of normal rainfall, despite immense pressure, anglers consistently catch trout up to 15 " in this lake. The inlet area has the best fly-fishing. Float tubers like this lake and they are usually able to catch trout from opening day until the close of the season, late afternoon and evening providing the fastest action as the summer passes.

Fly Fishing the middle section of the North Fork Snoqualmie River

North Fork Snoqualmie River (Map 2)

The North Fork is approximately 26 miles long. Along with the South and Middle Forks, it was stocked for many years with rainbow and cutthroat fry and catchables, as well as occasionally with eastern brook. Stocking was terminated in the early 1980's and it has been strictly a wild trout fishery since then. It is a medium size river, about midway between the Middle and South forks. The North Fork tends to be high early in the season and surveys have shown the best fishing to be in August and September. Anglers report the lower and middle stretches to yield the best success.

The lower North Fork is fishable upstream for about 2 miles from where it passes under the bridge on the County Road (Rd. 250), extending out of North Bend to Weyerhauser land, but you must wade and stay off the private land which borders it. Until it drops in late July and August, this section is difficult to wade without encroaching on private property. Holes and riffles are intermittent in this rather flat stretch of water and lots of walking is necessary to find holding areas. Nevertheless, this lower section is fished heavily just above the bridge for about a mile. There are fair numbers of rainbow and isolated cutthroat, both as large as 12-14." Although catch and release is not required, one should do so, because the trout

North Fork Snoqualmie River above the Black Canyon

population in the lower river is limited, very fragile and heavily fished.

From the bridge crossing the North Fork, the County Road travels by a number of homes on the river and heads sharply uphill past Ernie's Grove toward Weyerhauser land. Near the crest of the hill, there are several old logging roads allowing foot access to the river. A walk of about a mile will take you to the river, approximately 6 miles from its mouth, just above the Black Canyon. The river flows through the Black Canyon for about 4 miles, and enters the upper end of the private property section. Fishing is difficult and dangerous in the canyon, but some very cautious prospecting may get you to places seldom fished, in fine scenery. Above the Black Canyon, the river levels off and takes on a plunge pool, riffle and glide character for about 6 miles, extending all the way upstream to a concrete bridge crossing the North Fork on the County Road. The river is accessible here and there from the County Road by bushwhacking and from gated spur roads.

The Black Canyon, in keeping with seemingly all mysterious canyons, is reported to have some large trout hanging out in its very deep pools. The river upstream from the canyon to the concrete bridge has a few whitefish along with rainbow, cutthroat, and eastern brook. Most fish run 5-8" with some in the 10" range and a few to 12-14." Biologists know that trout to 16" can live in this river, as an angler was checked with such a cutthroat caught in the middle section not too long ago. There are reports of 20" trout from long ago.

Above the concrete bridge, the river meanders nearly 8 miles through a low gradient ancient lake bed. There are fine pools, riffles and brushy areas which

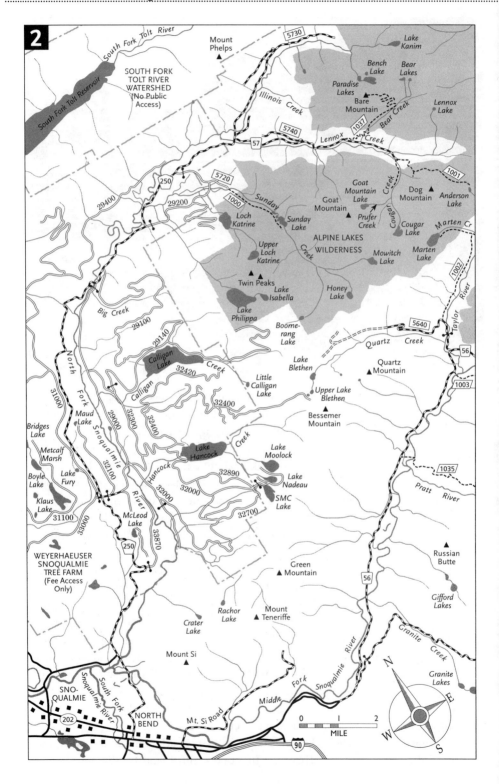

would seem to provide excellent habitat for larger trout but anglers find mainly cut-throat and brook trout to 10" with few larger. There are unfished beaver ponds here which harbor brookies and some cutthroat. The brookies predominate in the ponds and one can also find them here and there in the slower moving parts of the North Fork throughout its length. There is plenty of river to fish in this area and it is far less frequently fished than the stretch from the concrete bridge down to the mouth of the canyon.

The uppermost stretch of the river is quite small, cutting through a steep val-ley, seldom fished. It contains good numbers of small wild cutthroat, with an occa-sional 12" trout.

As to fly selection, there are seldom hatches on any of the Snoqualmie Forks which require a match for successful fly fishing. Standard dry flies such as Parachute Adams, Royal Wulf, Grey Wulf, or Elk Hair Caddis in size 14-10 will be all you will generally need if you can get the fish to rise, which is usually the case from mid-summer on. Beetles and Ants can also work well at times. Any standard nymph, such as Hare's Ear, Pheasant Tail, or caddis nymphs will do for subsurface fishing. These trout, with the exception of the largest, are seldom selective and a good presentation is the key to catching them.

Weyerhauser Land (Map 1, 2)

The Weyerhauser Co. has instituted a fee permit system for its large tract of land in the North Bend area. Payment of the annual permit fee allows access during specific hours throughout the year. There is very good lake and decent stream fish-ing in this area and the permit system has reduced the number of visitors. For resi-dents of the Puget Sound area, this is a bargain. Not only are there plenty of low-land lakes with trout, there are high mountain lakes which can be reached by bush-whacking or following old logging roads, and the North Fork Snoqualmie and the upper forks of the Tolt flow through this area providing enjoyable stream fishing. Many of the lakes are open all year and several have bass and perch as well as trout, allowing anglers to fish for plentiful spiny rays and trout in the same lake. (A tip: A veteran biologist once recommended a blue lure as surprisingly successful in the low Weyerhauser lakes.) One should always call ahead during fire-season because road closures can occur at any time. Maps may be obtained from Weyerhauser and are a must to find many of the lakes. (1- 800-433-3911)

Hull Lake (6 acres)

Hull is a large beaver-pond type lake in the East Fork Griffin Creek drainage. It is managed for stocked cutthroat in a quiet forest setting. Hull is fishable from shore, but best from a float tube or raft.

McLeod Lake (1006) (13 acres)

McLeod has long been known for its good fishing and offers regularly stocked rain-bow and resident eastern brook. It gets fished regularly, but holds up well. Anglers must walk in about five minutes on an unmarked abandoned road off the county road. A float tube or raft is needed since shoreline access is brushy and very difficult.

Klaus Lake (980) (62 acres)

Klaus is the lowermost of three interconnected lakes, including Boyle and Bridges. There is a rough 4x4 access on the lake's southeast corner. As a result of a study done by Bob Pfeifer of WDFW, all three are managed primarily for native cutthroat trout, with largemouth bass and yellow perch also present. They offer a nice opportunity to fish for spiny rays and trout in the same lake. There is fair to good fishing in all three lakes for cutthroat to 16." There is no stocking, so catch and release should be used with these wild cutthroat. If the trout are not biting, there is good fishing around the edges for smallmouth bass, mostly little but with a few lunkers, and perch to fair size. Bring some bass bugs and poppers along.

Boyle Lake (1040) (24 acres)

The middle of the three interconnected lakes, Boyle requires a short hike from a nearby spur road.

Bridges Lake (1045) (34 acres)

Bridges is the uppermost of the three interconnected lakes and is accessible by a short walk from nearby logging spurs.

Metcalf Marsh (1010) and (1040) (5 and 6 acres)

These small beaver-pond type lakes near Weyerhaeuser's mainline haul road have foot or car-topper access for stocked cutthroat trout.

Fury Lake (1005)

A Weyerhauser map will help you find this brushy 1 acre pond, stocked regularly with cutthroat. It also contains brook trout.

Black Lake (1213) (26 acres)

Boggy Black Lake has brookies and rainbow trout. It can provide fast fishing for 6-10" fish, with carry-overs to 16" or larger. It is stocked annually with rainbow. Access is by footpath from either the west or east off stubs from Weyerhaeuser's mainline haul road. Float tubes or small car-toppers must be packed a short distance to the lake.

Mud Lake (1270) (16 acres)

Mud Lake is a short way west of Weyerhaeuser's mainline road. Access is fair at best for small car-toppers or float tubes. Look for a primitive 4x4 path that leads to the lake's southern side. There is limited shore access, but the surroundings are sylvan and pleasant. Annual stocking provides good fishing for chunky rainbow, and an occasional carryover reported to several pounds. There are also eastern brook to 14."

Float-tube fishing is effective on Weyerhauser permit lakes.

Maud Lake   (2 acres)

Maud is sandwiched between the North Fork Snoqualmie River and Weyer-haeuser's Spur 10 logging road. A moderate bushwhack is required to reach the sometimes very good fishing for stocked coastal cutthroat, which grow to 14". A float tube or small raft is essential.

Lake Hancock (2172) (236 acres)

Hancock has a single small dirt access for car-toppers or light trailers at its north-west corner. Shoreline access is available, but is generally poor. The lake is set in thick woods and is accessible from several routes on Weyerhaeuser land. Like near-by Calligan Lake, Hancock offers an unusual assortment of rainbow, cutthroat and eastern brook, all now successfully reproducing and wild. All tributary streams and the upper third of the outlet are closed to fishing. It is popular with float tubers and contains some large trout. Catch and release should be practiced here. It is a good bet on a summer evening, providing both wet fly and dry fly anglers lots of water to explore and enough fish to make it very interesting.

Blethen Lakes

Both Blethen Lakes have historically been stocked with rainbow. The lower, 3 acre lake (3198) has fair natural reproduction and contains cutthroat and rainbow. 8 acre Upper Blethen (3665) depends upon regular stocking. A pothole in the area also con-tains trout. A Weyerhauser logging road once came within 250' of the upper lake.

The lakes may also be reached by a path and old trail from the end of Quartz Creek Rd. from the Taylor River area.

Lake Moolock (3903) Lake Nadeau (3722) and SMC (3702)

These three lakes, formerly popular with anglers and other visitors are presently inaccessible due to private land blocking access.

Calligan Lake (2222) (310 acres)

Calligan has a single rough access for car-toppers or light trailers midway down its north shore, plus extensive shoreline access. Calligan is reached from several routes and offers the same kind of quality fishery as Lake Hancock.

Little Calligan Lake (2700) (2 acres)

This small lake lies 1.5 miles up the southeast fork of the east inlet to Calligan Lake. It is basically an enlargement of the stream. There is no trail, but you can get to it by bushwhacking through in very brushy terrain in places. It is occasionally planted with rainbow and appears to have moderate natural reproduction. It has been reported to hold brookies as well.

Lake Phillipa (3346) (121 acres)

Phillipa is a large lake between Calligan and Loch Katrine. Old logging roads from Calligan Lake lead closest to Phillipa. While there was once a faint trail, a basically cross country slog of at least .75 mile through rough, brushy territory is required to reach the lake. It is periodically stocked with cutthroat or rainbow to augment its naturally reproducing cutthroat and rainbow and has long been known as a fine fishing lake.

Lake Isabella (3510) (12.5 acres)

Isabella Lies at the head of the inlet to Phillipa and can be reached if you can find Phillipa first and work your way to its inlet. There is no established trail between the two but it is only about an hour scramble from the inlet. It has historically been regularly stocked with rainbow.

Sunday Creek Area   (Map 2)

Follow the County Road up the North Fork Snoqualmie River approximately 14 miles until it crosses Sunday Creek and continue to gated rd. 5720 off to the right. Walk about one mile on the old road, bypassing a spur road to the left. You will then find a fork, take the left fork to the creek. The trailhead to Sunday Lake begins here. The right fork also leads across the river, to a beaten path leading to an old logging road uphill to Loch Katrine. Records indicate that once upon a time, grayling were stocked in the creek but they did not take. It is closed to fishing to allow wild cutthroat to spawn and repopulate the North Fork Snoqualmie. If it reopens, catch and release is imperative to maintain the population of wild cutts.

Loch Katrine

Loch Katrine (3000) (51) acres

In addition to reaching Loch Katrine by the Sunday Creek route, one can walk to it by parking at a gated logging road and trudging up the road approximately 2.5 miles. There is a lovely island in the lake, which is very brushy and requires a good deal of thrashing about to reach good casting spots. It contains now wild and self-sustaining small to good size rainbow which anglers can help keep that way by releasing all you catch or keeping no more than one. If you can stand to haul it, a float tube is helpful here. This is a good place to catch a wild rainbow early in the season.

Upper Loch Katrine (4250) (24 acres)

This remote high mountain lake is reached only by difficult cross-country hiking through deep woods south from Loch Katrine or west and steeply west-southwest uphill from Sunday Lake. It has been historically stocked with either rainbow or golden trout and produces 13-15" fish.

Sunday Lake (1865) (21 acres)

A connected series of brushy ponds, just within the Alpine Lakes Wilderness, Sunday Lake produces small to a few large cutthroat, particularly in mid-to-late-summer for skilled anglers. It is regularly stocked with cutthroat. The hike, which begins at gated rd. 5720, is 2.6 miles on an easy grade but requires fording Sunday Creek. The lake may fluctuate widely in size in drought years, and is best fished

Weyerhauser High Lake Rainbow Trout

from a raft. It fills with snow melt and can be very full and cold early, making casting tough and fishing difficult.

Bushwhackers seeking more remote spots in the Sunday Creek area, find in about 1.5 miles up Sunday Creek south of Sunday Lake, that it forks in three directions. At the head of the west fork is **Boomerang Lake** (3215) (1 acre), thought to be barren. **Mowitch Lake** (3196) (16 acres) is the headwater of the east fork. There was once a trail but now access is by bushwhacking up the creek and east fork for 2.75 miles from Sunday Lake, elevation gain 2300′ or cross-country from an old logging road off Quartz Creek trail, which begins up the Taylor River Rd. in the Middle Fork Snoqualmie area. Rainbow apparently spawn successfully in the more westerly of the lake's two inlet streams. **Honey Lake** (3233) (9 acres) is the source of the middle fork of Sunday Creek. Access is just over a mile up the middle fork of Sunday Creek, about a 2.5 mile bushwhack from Sunday Lake with no trail. It is regularly stocked with rainbow. All three lakes may also possibly be reached cross-country from the Quartz Creek trail off the Taylor River Rd. but this could be a treacherous route. The lakes are seldom visited.

Lennox Creek Area (Map 2)

Continue on the main County Road past the fork to Sunday Creek and Sunday Lakes trail, bearing right at the next major fork, soon crossing Lennox Creek.

Bear Lakes (4850)

There are three shallow meadow lakes, one 3 acres and two potholes above, on the south side of a 5300′ peak, called by some Bear Mt., due west of Bare Mt. The potholes contain a fragile population of self-sustaining cutthroat trout. There is also occasional rainbow stocking in the lake. Take Bear Creek trail off Lennox Creek Rd. past the fork to Bare Mt. lookout and continue about .6 mile to where it crosses Bear Creek. From here, bushwhack near the stream 1 mile to the lake. At one time, at the fork to Bare Mt., an old boot track led to the ruins of a miner's cabin, where a trail led to the lake and beyond.

Lennox Lake (5000) (2 acres)

A small lake on a rocky ridge 1 mile southeast of Bear Lakes, this remote lake requires a cross-country, very tough struggle from a number of directions. There is a nearby pothole. Both are periodically stocked with rainbow.

Paradise Lakes (4050) (5 and 23 acres)

Just north of the saddle between Bear Mt. and Bare Mt., lie Paradise Lakes. Take the Bear Creek trail for 2 miles, then Bare Mt. trail to the lakes. These meadow lakes are connected by streams, along with **Bench Lake** (4180) (25 acres). All are said to contain cutthroat, through natural reproduction. There have also been reports of eastern brook. The Paradise Lakes have been periodically stocked with rainbow.

Goat Mt. Lake (4117) (10 acres)

Goat Mt. Lake, also known as Prufer and Little Cougar, is a pretty mountain tarn circled by rock slides and alpine timber. Bushwhack up Cougar Creek from Lennox Creek Rd., then right 1 mile up a small creek, Prufer Creek, named for an old miner who used to keep people out. The lake has naturally reproducing cutthroat with good fishing. Rainbow and golden trout have also been stocked from time to time. **Big Cougar Lake** (4123) (20 acres) lies one mile south of Goat Mountain Lake and .75 mile northwest of Marten Lake and is best accessed from Marten, as its outlet stream is impassable, appropriately named Devil's Canyon. It may also be accessible from the Dog Mt. trail. Either way is a mean bushwhack. The presence of trout depends entirely on stocking, as there is no suitable habitat for spawning. It is unknown whether it presently contains trout.

Lake Kamin (4000) (18 acres)

The headwater of the North Fork Snoqualmie River, very scenic and very isolated, Kamin is 1 mile northeast of Bench Lake. Not accessible by trail, it lies cross-country from Bench, Bear and Paradise Lakes. It is extremely difficult as well as dangerous to reach. It is reported to have a small population of self-sustaining cutthroat.

Anderson Lake (4300) (2 acres)

Tr. 1001 from end of Lennox Creek Rd. leads 3.8 miles to the lake, steeply for the first two miles, then on an easier grade, a 1900' elevation gain in all. The lake is frequently fished and is regularly stocked with rainbow, topping out at 12-14."

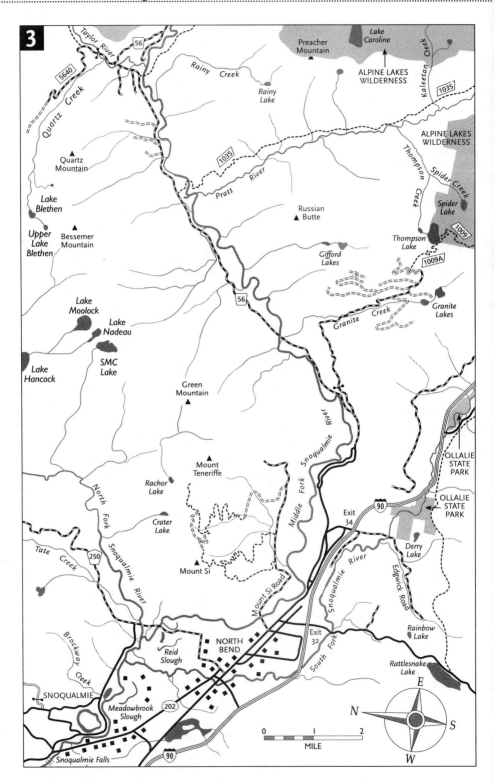

Middle Fork Snoqualmie River Area (Map 3, 4)

The Middle Fork Snoqualmie River has long been a very popular area for anglers and hikers. The river extends 40 miles from its source to meet the North and South Forks just outside North Bend. Numerous side roads and trails take off from the Middle Fork Rd., making it a major route for hiking to lakes in the area.

Middle Fork Snoqualmie River

The Middle Fork is a truly exquisite mountain river, so close to cities and suburbs (about 45 minutes from Seattle) but so far away when you are alone on it. Among all of the very scenic rivers in Western Washington, to many, it is the most beautiful. From its headwaters it flows through steep valleys abutting ridges over 6000', slow-moving stretches, high gradient fast flowing boulder reaches, a broad mountain valley, and finally to its junction with the South and North Forks. State and local governments were asleep when applications were filed to build houses alongside it in some of its lower reaches and there are more than a few next to the lower section of the Middle Fork. You can't blame anyone for wanting to live in such a place, but the public interest was utterly ignored in the process. One can only hope that the river is not unduly degraded. It deserves complete protection from its headwaters to its junction with the North and South Forks, both of which merit equal protection before they are lost as wild, natural mountain rivers.

First access to the Middle Fork is at a bridge on the County Road out of North Bend just before it crosses the North Fork. One can wade upstream from here after runoff subsides, being careful to stay off private property, which surrounds the river. The holes are far apart and lots of walking is necessary to reach good spots in this low gradient section of the river. Above this area, there is access from Mt. Si Rd. as it crosses the river and follows it through what has unbelievably become a residential area. There is also access to the lower river from the old road leading into North Bend from Edgewick Rd. Once you're legitimately in the river, you can wade it and its shoreline upstream or down.

To fish the middle section, take exit 34 on I-90, cross under the freeway, drive through Truck Town, and find Edgewick Rd. leading upstream for access to about 16 miles of river, to the Taylor River Rd. and beyond, until your vehicle cannot take it, or to the road end. It is likely the road will be closed at Dingford Creek in the near future. Dingford Creek is about 25 river miles up the Middle Fork.

The first 3 or 4 miles of the river up this road are very difficult to reach without crossing private property. Once above the residential section, there are miles of river to fish with unlimited access. It is best to bushwhack, as the river gets fished regularly next to the road and one does better where it is seldom fished. WDFW studies have shown the average size of trout to be larger .25 mile from places easily reached. The Edgewick Rd. section of the river has truly beautiful scenery but the average size of fish is slightly smaller than the lower and upper stretches.

The Middle Fork trail affords access to sections of the river not often fished. Not

Healthy Middle Fork Snoqualmie River Rainbow

only does an angler get away from roadside fishing spots by walking the trail a bit, he or she can fish the side of the river not fished by the vast majority, who get out of the car and head to the river. The trail begins .5 miles before the Taylor River bridge, crossing the Middle Fork on a bridge and heading upstream for about 11 miles, past Goldmeyer Hot Springs. There is another bridge crossing back over the Middle Fork at Dingford Creek, about 5 miles upstream.

At the point Dingford Creek enters the river, there is very good pocket water fishing. A trail leads from here up the Middle Fork to the Alpine Lakes Wilderness and hikers are rewarded with pristine fishing in crystalline water for many miles, clear up to the point where the river becomes creek size.

The river tends to be high and a bit cloudy until midsummer, and it is very difficult wading, as it seems to have been created to contain as many large rocks and boulders of varying size as possible, all covered with slippery silt from runoff.

Some years ago, Washington restricted the Middle Fork and its main tributaries, Pratt River and Taylor River, to strictly catch and release fishing. After considerable study, biologists concluded that with a no-kill fishery, eventually the river will support at least fair numbers of 15- 16" cutthroat spread throughout good holding areas. Part of this conclusion was based upon verified historical catches of 16" cutthroat, with some reliably reported to 20" in the 1950's, and it has been consistently found that the largest trout in the Middle Fork are cutthroat. It is also felt that the river will slowly become almost entirely a wild cutthroat stream, as numbers of rainbow and hybrids have been found to be fairly low, except in the Dingford area, despite decades of stocking.

After the change to catch and release, Middle Fork anglers gradually began to report slightly larger average size trout with some cutthroat reaching 14-15". Though somewhat suspect because anglers always add at least 1-3" to the trout they catch, it is widely accepted that there are increasing numbers of older, larger trout in the river.

In the lower river, one can find more 12-14" trout, with cutthroat nearly all the large ones. The holes and pockets are full of small trout as well and dry fly fishing can be very enjoyable. An Elk Hair Caddis or Royal Wulf, size 10-14 will nearly always bring trout up from their lairs in mid to late summer, with a Parachute Adams a reliable fly at any time dry flies are working. The larger trout are typically more difficult to entice to dry flies and a dropper with a Hare's Ear, Pheasant Tail, or a caddis nymph may bring more takes from those reluctant 12"+ trout. The Edgewick Rd. section of the river seems somewhat less productive than the lower and upper sections but it is very scenic and worth plenty of fishing time. Above and just below Dingford Creek, there is very good pocket water fishing for slightly larger trout, predominately rainbow, with a 12" trout not too rare. There are few if any 14" trout though. There have been reports of golden trout caught in the river here, probably fish that migrated downstream from a high lake. The Dingford area is fishable fairly early, but until the river drops later in the summer, it takes "hand on root, knee on rock" wading and bushwhacking to cover much ground.

A few miles upstream from Dingford Creek, the stretches near the road/trail are infrequently fished due to road conditions and hiking distances but they are truly pristine, with historically rumors of big fish, as always, coming from those remote reaches. There are nearly 14 more miles of river to fish above Dingford Creek, most of it accessible by road and trail. Here and there one comes across deep pools and holding areas with good numbers of 12-14" trout, some larger.

Granite Lakes

A few miles up the Middle Fork Rd., just past the last of the pavement and houses built foolishly and unwisely next to the river, an old logging road leads uphill to the right and is gated in less than a mile. Beyond here, a maze of roads leads in roughly 4.5 miles to these two lakes, both of which can provide good fishing. They are usually ice-free by June, sometimes in May. **Upper Granite Lake** (3060) (15 acres) has a small number of naturally sustaining rainbow supplemented by occasional stocking. **Lower Granite Lake** (2950) (9 acres) is regularly stocked with rainbow. Both contain sizable rainbow. The gated road prevents automobiles from driving to the lake but trail bikers, walkers and mountain bikers find their way through the complicated road system to the lakes. Not long ago, a developer bought an inholding on the lakes and attempted to develop it, including reopening and regrading the road. This was opposed by many parties, including WDFW. **Granite Creek** has an abundant supply of small brook trout.

Thompson Lake (3650) (47 acres)

Continue on the logging road beyond the cutoff to the Granite Lakes to an old trailhead leading 1 mile over a ridge and down to Thompson Lake. There is also trail access from Little Mason Lake .5 miles beyond Mason Lake on Mason Lake trail, by tr. 1009 another 4.4 miles to Thompson. Some self-sustaining rainbow/cutthroat are supplemented by occasional rainbow plants. This productive lake is known to produce trout to 17-18." The remains of an old miner cabin may be found on the east shore.

Spider Lake (2746) (15 acres)

Southeast less than a mile and downhill from Thompson Lake, Spider lies in a deep trough on the north side of Mt. Defiance. There is no trail access and no good place to camp at the lake. It has a self-sustaining cutthroat population, with anglers finding trout of all ages and size.

Gifford Lakes (3200) (12 acres and 4 acres)

These two lakes used to be readily accessible but with the gating of the logging road to Granite Lake, it takes a long walk on a confusing road system to find a way to get to the lakes. They have become remote, in a nice valley setting. Both lakes are reported to have successfully spawning rainbow.

Pratt River

An old trail heads 8 miles up the Pratt River, but crossing the Middle Fork Snoqualmie River can only be accomplished in late summer or fall. The trail is in tough shape in spots as it is seldom used. Fish the river a ways up for small cutts, a few rainbow and some eastern brook. A 12" trout is a lunker in the Pratt, but you will seldom see anyone else, there are no vehicles and you will be alone in the valley with the river. There are beaver ponds in the middle and upper Pratt which rarely see anglers but have been reported by wily veteran anglers to have great fishing at times. The river is catch and release only.

Rainy Lake (3764) (5 acres)

A small lake in rock and timber 1 mile northwest of Shamrock Lakes, Rainy's outlet enters the Middle Fork just west of the mouth of the Taylor River. Upper Rainy Lake lies at 3900' just east of Rainy Lake in timber. Rainy, with good spawning habitat, produces now wild cutthroat, occasionally supplemented by stocking, generally rainbow.

Taylor River

Some time ago, a road paralleled the Taylor River for a long distance and was heavily traveled by automobiles. Now it is gated and slowly turning into a path. Hikers may find company from people on bikes. The river is readily accessible in many places and contains small cutthroat and rainbow. It is a no bait, catch and release fishery. As always, the farther one walks, generally the less the river has seen anglers. The road/trail is the gateway to many lakes, including a few that open by mid to late May.

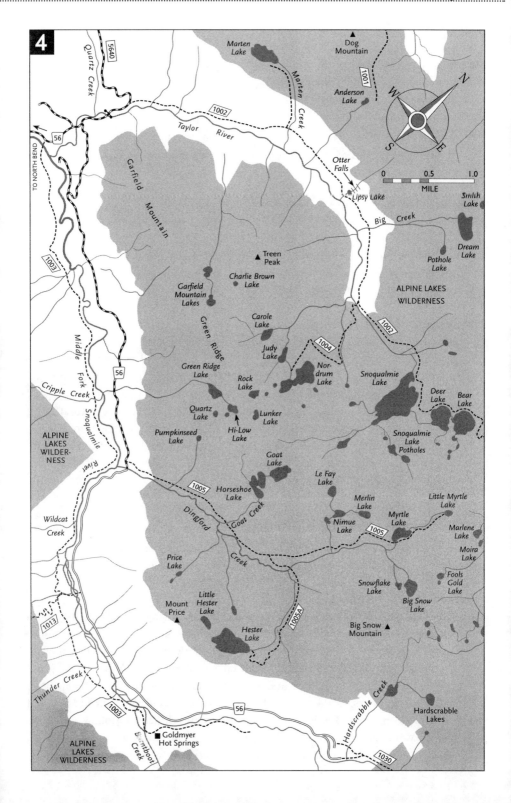

4

Quartz Creek

5640

1002

Taylor River

TO NORTH BEND

56

1003

56

Garfield Mountain

Middle Fork

Cripple Creek

Snoqualmie River

ALPINE LAKES WILDERNESS

Wildcat Creek

1013

Thunder Creek

1003

ALPINE LAKES WILDERNESS

Marten Lake

Dog Mountain

1001

Anderson Lake

Marten Creek

Otter Falls

Lipsy Lake

Big Creek

Sitlih Lake

Dream Lake

Pothole Lake

ALPINE LAKES WILDERNESS

Treen Peak

Charlie Brown Lake

Garfield Mountain Lakes

Green Ridge

Carole Lake

Judy Lake

1004

Nordrum Lake

Snoqualmie Lake

Deer Lake

Bear Lake

1002

Green Ridge Lake

Rock Lake

Quartz Lake

Lunker Lake

Hi-Low Lake

Pumpkinseed Lake

Snoqualmie Lake Potholes

Goat Lake

Le Fay Lake

Merlin Lake

Little Myrtle Lake

Horseshoe Lake

1005

Dingford

Goat Creek

Nimue Lake

Myrtle Lake

1005

Marlene Lake

Moira Lake

Price Lake

Creek

Fools Gold Lake

Little Hester Lake

Snowflake Lake

Big Snow Lake

Mount Price

1005A

Hester Lake

Big Snow Mountain

Hardscrabble Creek

Hardscrabble Lakes

56

Goldmyer Hot Springs

Burntboot Creek

1030

N
W E
S

0   0.5   1.0
MILE

Marten Lake (2959) (40 acres)

Drive .4 mile up the Taylor River Rd. from the Middle Fork Rd. to the gate. At 3 miles up the road, just before a small wooden bridge crosses Marten Creek, a rough, rocky, trail begins, dropping then heading straight up without switchbacks, to the left, 1.5 miles to this brushy lake, 1900' gain. Self-sustaining rainbow, spawning in a beautiful inlet, tending toward 9-10"' inhabit the lake. The outlet flows over an unusual series of small rock waterfalls. Marten is often fishable by mid-May but the trout can be finicky, feeding on chironomids early on. Limit your take or practice catch and release to allow this lake to maintain its now wild trout.

Lipsy Lake (1900)

This very small lake, really a pond, is a consistent producer of cutthroat, mostly small. Hike the Taylor River road/trail from the gate to approximately 1 mile beyond the turnoff to Marten Lake, about 4 total miles. Lipsy is the site of beautiful Otter Falls. Lipsy's outlet stream crosses the trail and the lake is easily located 200' from the trail.

Dream Lake (3400) (35 acres)

Big Creek crosses the Taylor River trail approximately .5 mile beyond Lipsy Lake. For years, anglers have been getting up to this lake from here, approximately 1 mile, 1550' gain, by a rough trail and rugged bushwhack. It is not recommended until snow melt is finished for the season. Big Creek's left fork as one heads uphill leads to the lake, which is regularly stocked and usually has lots of 10-11" fish, depending upon the stocking cycle. It has a nice little island. The right fork comes from **Pothole Lake** (3900) (3 acres), which is directly south 1500' from the south side of Dream lake. It is reported to have a small number of reproducing rainbow/cutthroat.

Smith Lake (4500) (2 acres)

This small, glacier fed lake in alpine country, with beautiful blue-green water, is found through a pass east of Dream Lake, then contouring northwest, about 6 hours from the Taylor River Rd. gate. It is periodically planted with rainbow.

Nordrum Lake (3700) (60 acres)

Nordrum is the largest lake in an area of real interest to anglers. It has self-sustaining rainbow/cutthroat, supplemented by periodic stocking. The Trail Blazers once had a cabin here. It is relatively easy to fish from shore and was heavily fished when the Taylor River Rd. was not gated. It now takes a hike of 9 miles from the trailhead, 2500' gain. Just beyond the fork in the Taylor River trail leading left to Snoqualmie and Dorothy Lakes, at the end of the old roadbed, a trail takes off to Nordrum uphill a steep, rocky 3 miles, 2000' gain, sometimes difficult to follow and quite rough. Mountain goat types have beaten their way in to Nordrum via Green Ridge, via an old faint trail beginning approximately 150 yards west of where Green Ridge

Lake's outlet stream crosses the Middle Fork Rd. from the north, about 1 mile before the road reaches Dingford Creek.

From Nordrum, anglers can wander cross-country for days to other good fishing. Faint trails lead to rainbow stocked **Rock Lake** (3860), a productive lake .25 mile southwest of the south end of Nordrum, with its unique enormous boulder field outlet; **Lunker Lake** (4300) (3.5 acres), southeast .2 mile of Rock Lake, also rainbow stocked, with some really respectable size fish; **Hi Low Lake** (4100) (4 acres), stocked with rainbow; **Green Ridge Lake** (4200) (15.5 acres) with naturally reproducing cutthroat/rainbow, some large, fed by the outlet stream from Hi Low Lake; and **Quartz Lake** (4100) (1 acre) occasionally planted with cutthroat, but sometimes subject to winter-kill, which is southwest from the southernmost shore of Hi Low, past a small pothole, on a ridge, about .3 mile in all from Hi Low. **Pumpkin Seed Lake** (4270), a very small lake set off by itself, is .75 mile south of Quartz Lake and is stocked with rainbow, a producer of some big fish. It is also accessible from the Myrtle Lake trail.

Nearby to the west of Nordrum, brushy **Judy Lake** (3600) (10 acres) occasionally stocked with rainbow to supplement its self-sustaining rainbow/cutthroat, is fed by the intermittent outlet of Nordrum, and is a very difficult descent from Nordrum. The inlet at Judy is spectacular, with high flows at times causing Judy's waters to exchange three or four times a year and feeding highly charged underwater springs. Trout may be spawning on the rubble and sand "beaches"produced adjacent to the springs. The lake supports good numbers of medium sized rainbow. Rainbow stocked **Carole Lake** (3700) (11 acres) lies .25 west and drains north to Judy. Carole reportedly has some reproducing cutthroat and rainbow, with respectable size trout. **Garfield Mt. Lakes** (4500) and (4000) (8 acres lower, 7 upper) are located in beautiful alpine country on the northeast side of Garfield Mt. Mountain goats have frequently been seen in the area. The lower lake, which is stocked with rainbow, is .25 mile down the outlet stream. The upper lake has reproducing cutthroat, rainbow and cuttbows to 14" and better. The lakes are very remote and a difficult cross-country trek west from Carole Lake, or 3 grueling miles up their outlet stream from where it enters the Taylor River. **Charlie Brown Lake** (4300) (2 acres) is a small lake in rocky country on the southwest side of Treen Peak. Its outlet stream flows into the stream connecting the Garfield Lakes. It has very limited and intermittent successful spawning and depends upon stocking to consistently produce trout. It has a good food supply and is reported to have good numbers of impressive trout.

Dingford Creek Area   (Map 4, 5)
Horseshoe Lake (3900) (25 acres)

Take the Dingford Creek trail about 2 miles to a fisherman's trail north up Goat Creek, staying on the east side of the creek, 1 mile uphill, 900' gain. Horseshoe has been known to produce old, wise and tough to catch, large rainbow, both self-sustaining and periodically stocked.

Goat Lake (4100) (19.5 acres)

Follow the small inlet to Horseshoe Lake .2 mile upstream to Goat. It is reported to hold large fish.

Myrtle Lake (3950) (18 acres)

After an initial stiff uphill hike, the Dingford Creek trail flattens and splits at 3.5 miles. Take the left fork another 4 miles, 800' gain to this popular lake, where now natural rainbow/cutthroat are periodically supplemented with stocked rainbow. It is a familiar base camp for anglers exploring the area. **Little Myrtle Lake** (4400) (4 acres), also occasionally stocked, is found about 1 mile above via a trail on the west side of the creek at the north end of Myrtle. From here, anglers can reach two more rainbow or cutthroat planted lakes, **Marlene Lake** (3900) (3 acres) and **Moira Lake** (4000) (5 acres) by route-finding, continuing northeasterly .5 through a notch, then slightly east. Good fishing has been reported in each. Both lakes are also accessible by bushwhacking up their outlet streams which flow into the south end of Lake Dorothy.

There are 3 other lakes cross-country within .5 to 1 mile southwest of Myrtle, with no trail access. **Merlin Lake (4000)** (6 acres), is a shallow meadow lake, periodically stocked and known historically to produce large trout at times; **Nimue Lake** (4000) (25 acres), which is reported to have a good population of naturally reproducing rainbow/cutthroat, mostly small to medium size, along with a pothole in its outlet; and **LeFay Lake** (4100) (7 acres) which is rainbow stocked.

Big Snow Lake (5000) (15 acres)

The source of the North Fork of Dingford Creek, lying on the north side of Big Snow Mt., this mountain lake is an exceptional beauty. There is no trail to it and it lies cross-country from Myrtle Lake trail, approximately 7 miles from the trailhead. It has naturally reproducing cutthroat and is reported to have golden trout. A small pond to the south of Myrtle Lake is adjacent to Big Snow's outlet stream. Seven other lakes are nearby, including **Snowflake Lake,** (4840) (3 acres), close by to the southwest, and **Fools Gold Lake** (4900) (3 acres) north of Big Snow but tougher to get to, uphill east from Big Snow's east shore, northeast then north. Both lakes were stocked at one time, Fools Gold with golden trout but it is not known whether they now contain trout.

Hester Lake (4050) (67 acres)

At 3.5 miles, the Dingford Creek trail leads via its right fork another often muddy and sometimes tough to find 2 miles to Hester, a cirque lake at the foot of Mt. Price.

Hester Lake

This popular lake is a steady producer of stocked rainbow, supplementing very limited numbers of naturally reproducing trout. **Little Hester Lake** (4200) (9.5 acres) west just above, at the head of Hester's inlet stream, is regularly stocked, either with rainbow or goldens. A small unnamed lake lies northwest over a ridge from Hester.

Hardscrabble Lakes (4550) (8 acres upper and 10 acres lower)

These two alpine lakes lie at the foot of Big Snow Mt. in very scenic country. There is no formal trail access. At Dingford Creek, do a little fishing in the Middle Fork Snoqualmie. Then hike 6.5 miles to near the Dutch Miller trailhead, or drive the old Middle Fork Rd. as far as your vehicle can go, then walk to the same point, roughly .5 miles before the road ends. Here an old road starts uphill. Find within 400-500 feet a footpath which travels 1200' uphill north about 1.5 miles toward the lakes, paralleling Hardscrabble Creek on its west side, eventually to the lower lake. The upper lake is .5 mile farther up the left side of the east inlet by a fair trail. Both provide good habitat for spawning cutthroat/rainbow. Potholes in the area may also contain trout.

Upper Hardscrabble Lake

Avalanche Lake (3780) (3 acres)

Two lakes head up Burntboot drainage. Access is extremely difficult and said to be dangerous. One described route is from the break-off point on the Pacific Crest Trail coming from the Mineral Creek trail. Another is from the end of the Middle Fork Rd. Avalanche was planted with rainbow some time ago. **Iceberg Lake (4850) (21 acres)** is a beautiful mountain cirque one mile farther up Burnt Boot Creek. Iceberg's outlet is an 800' falls. This glacier fed lake is appears to be virtually inaccessible but is reported to have been planted with golden trout at one time.

Overcoat Lake (5900) (14 acres)

A very high, rarely visited lake on the northwest side of glacier-clad Overcoat Peak, Overcoat's outlet plunges 2500' in one mile to meet the Middle Fork Snoqualmie from the south. It is an extremely remote lake but has been stocked on occasion.

Williams Lake (4500) (15 acres)

Spectacularly set, this lake is reached by driving to the end of the Middle Fork Rd., beyond Dingford Creek 6 miles to Hardscrabble Creek, if the road is passable, you have lots of patience and your vehicle is able. From here, hike along the Middle Fork and fish as you choose. Historically, there have been reports of large trout high up on the Middle Fork where it flattens out, about 5-6 miles in. Pedro Camp is located at 6 miles, 4100' an easy 1100' gain. Shortly, a fork in the trail leads left and

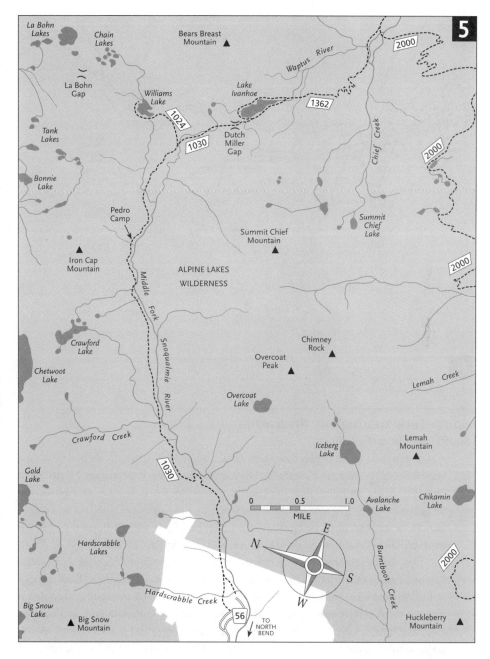

upward to Williams Lake, about 1.5 miles from Pedro Camp. The lake can also be reached from the Skykomish area and from Waptus Lake. Although it has great potential, it is believed to be barren because of old mining activities. Stocked trout have never survived in the past. Pedro Pond has naturally spawning cutthroat. Above Williams, from its northeast corner are the Chain Lakes.

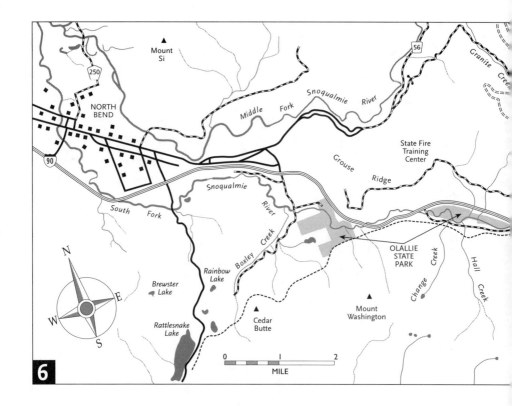

South Fork Snoqualmie River Area (Map 6, 7)
South Fork Snoqualmie River

Thousands of cars pass the South Fork Snoqualmie River on their way across Snoqualmie Pass, as it runs parallel to I-90 literally down the Pass through North Bend. Flowing nearly 36 miles from its headwaters at Source Lake, the smallest of the Snoqulamie forks, it is also the most impacted by development. Flood control measures have resulted in its being diked for several miles as well. It flows through the town of North Bend to meet the other forks near Reinig Rd.

Despite the impacts upon it, some fishermen claim the South Fork has the best fly-fishing of any of the forks. It has for many years been a no-bait barbless hook fishery with catch and size limits, but not a catch and release river. It is interesting to compare it to the catch and release Middle Fork. Some argue that the South Fork is the richer fork, that trout tend to be about an inch longer on average and that catch and release might only increase the number of small trout. Others consider this heresy, contending that catch and release would result in more fish surviving to old age, and thus allowing for larger trout.

The South Fork is the most accessible of the three Snoqualmie Forks and also easier to wade, as it is smaller, about ½ the flow of the Middle Fork, shallower and easier to cross, generally has quite a bit of small rock and gravel and is not very silty.

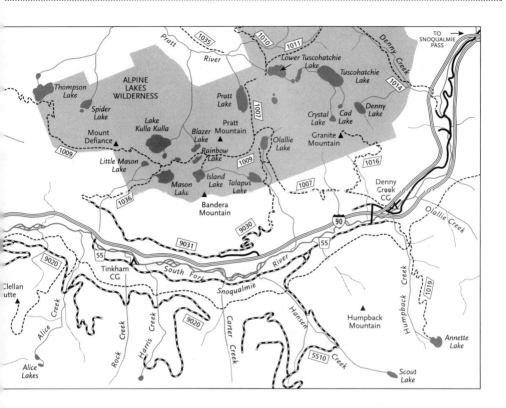

In most places, it can be fished by wading straight upstream with relative ease once it drops in volume.

The lower reaches in the North Bend area contain fair numbers of rainbow, cutthroat, hybridized cuttbows, whitefish and an occasional eastern brook. While most fish are small, a few 11-13" trout inhabit the lower river. The rip-rapped areas, where boulders have created riffles and pools, can be surprisingly good fishing, if one can ignore freeway noise. The middle stretches above North Bend are further distant from the freeway, more difficult to get to and resultingly have a few more fish, with the average size a bit larger. 12-14" cutthroat and rainbow are not common but there are enough to intrigue anyone used to fishing for typical 6-9" South Fork trout.

The upper South Fork, visible alongside I-90 for miles, drops to very low volume in mid to late summer and fall and becomes creek size. Nevertheless, there are lots of 6-8" fish and an occasional surprise 12-14" rainbow or cutthroat. Brookies are increasingly found upstream, but there are a few in the lower and middle stretches of the river.

Above the Denny Creek/Asaheal Curtis exit, early in the summer when the river has a robust flow, there is fair to good fishing for cutthroat. Once it begins to drop substantially, there is little to recommend for fishermen except isolated pockets and deep pools.

Due to population pressures, there has been far too much residential development next to the river and unless you seek out the more remote sections, you may find yourself fishing next to homes, along with folks swimming, tubing, relaxing in lawn chairs and recreating in a variety of ways which make fishing the South Fork more of an urban fishing experience. Fishermen must be vocal to protect the South Fork from any further development.

There is no specific fly to recommend when fishing the South Fork. For dry fly anglers, an Adams is good in early and late summer, Royal Wulf and Elk Hair Caddis the rest of the time. Terrestrials are good later in the summer. When the trout won't rise, any standard nymph pattern will bring better results, such as a Hare's Ear or Pheasant Tail. There are good numbers of caddis in the South Fork, so a caddis nymph can be a good searching nymph.

Mason Lake/Talapus Lake Area

The area containing Mason Lake east to Talapus Lake is surely one of the most heavily used mountain tracts in the Washington State. It is very easy to reach from the greater Seattle/Eastside area and provides relatively easy access to a number of alpine lakes. Many are short day hikes. Despite this, some of the lakes have good fishing and a little extra effort, particularly overnight hiking, allows anglers a nice fishing experience for mountain trout. Loop trips are possible as well. However, if you want to avoid crowds, other anglers, and other hikers, go on weekdays or spend the time to get to a more remote area. The area has so many visitors that restrictions are probable in the future. As always, leave no trace.

Mason Lake (4180) (33 acres)

From I-90 exit 45 to the north leads to rd. 9030 and the Mason Lake trailhead. Walk the abandoned road .75 mile then uphill a rather miserable, boulder strewn 1.75 miles steeply to the lake, an elevation gain of 2000' from the trailhead. Caution is advised on this heavily traveled trail, as a few people have met their end in falls from it. Once at the lake, you are within one mile of four other lakes. Mason has an open shoreline and is easily fished. It is regularly stocked with rainbow, has historically been a good fishing lake, with a few lunkers to 18" reported.

Little Mason Lake (4200) (4 acres)

Take off west shortly after passing Mason Lake and in .3 mile, sometimes quite brushy and muddy, find Little Mason, which is regularly stocked with rainbow.

Kulla Kulla Lake (3765) (60 acres)

From the trail junction about .5 mile beyond Mason Lake, Kulla Kulla lies north downhill by way trail .6 mile, through rocks generously endowed with devil's club. It is also reachable from the Talapus Lake/ Pratt Lake trail system. A few naturally reproducing rainbow/cutthroat are supplemented with occasional rainbow stocking and the lake generally has trout 6-15." Mountain goats are sometimes seen in this area. Deep **Little Kulla Kulla (3800) (3 acres)** feeds its much larger sister lake from the south and holds cutthroat.

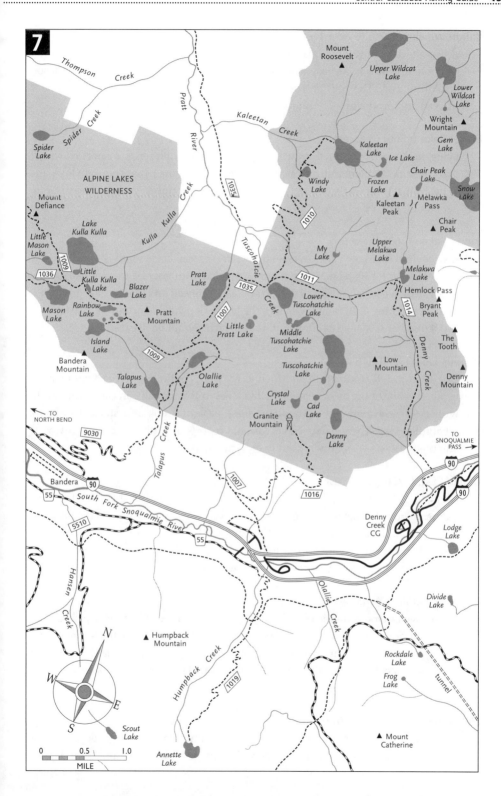

7

Thompson Creek

Spider Creek

Pratt River

Kaleetan Creek

Mount Roosevelt

Upper Wildcat Lake

Lower Wildcat Lake

Wright Mountain

Gem Lake

Spider Lake

Kulla Kulla Creek

ALPINE LAKES WILDERNESS

Mount Defiance

Lake Kulla Kulla

Little Mason Lake

1036 1009

Little Kulla Kulla Lake

Blazer Lake

Mason Lake

Rainbow Lake

Pratt Mountain

Island Lake

Bandera Mountain

1009

Talapus Lake

Olallie Lake

Pratt Lake

1035

1007

Little Pratt Lake

Tuscohatchie Creek

1010

1011

Kaleetan Lake

Ice Lake

Windy Lake

Frozen Lake

My Lake

Upper Melakwa Lake

Kaleetan Peak

Chair Peak Lake

Melawka Pass

Snow Lake

Chair Peak

Melakwa Lake

Hemlock Pass

1014

Bryant Peak

Lower Tuscohatchie Lake

Middle Tuscohatchie Lake

Tuscohatchie Lake

The Tooth

Denny Creek

Denny Mountain

Low Mountain

Crystal Lake

Cad Lake

Granite Mountain

Denny Lake

TO NORTH BEND

9030

Talapus Creek

1007

Bandera

90

55

South Fork Snoqualmie River

5510

55

TO SNOQUALMIE PASS

90

1016

Denny Creek CG

Lodge Lake

90

Hansen Creek

N

W   E

S

Humpback Mountain

Humpback Creek

1019

Olallie Creek

Divide Lake

Rockdale Lake

Frog Lake

tunnel

Scout Lake

Annette Lake

Mount Catherine

0   0.5   1.0
MILE

Rainbow Lake (4270) (6 acres)

A heavily fished meadow lake, approximately 1 mile east of the Mason Lake trail junction, Rainbow is an easy walk from the junction, 4 miles in all from the Mason Lake Trailhead. The trail passes a small pond on the way. The lake is regularly stocked and produces 9-11" rainbow with an occasional holdover lunker.

Blazer Lake (4060) (6 acres)

Lying in a meadow directly north of Rainbow Lake, Blazer is a short downhill descent from the main trail or a steeper one from Rainbow Lake. There are lily pads in the lake. It is regularly planted with rainbow and produces variable sizes of trout, depending upon the stocking cycle.

Island Lake (4260) (17 acres)

Just beyond Rainbow Lake, an essentially flat side trail leads south .4 mile to Island Lake. Named for its picturesque miniature island with gnarled trees, it is basically midway between Talapus trailhead, Pratt Lake trailhead and Mason Lake trailhead. Regular stocking with rainbow makes the lake a dependable producer. It also has a small number of self-sustaining cutthroat, which should be released.

Talapus Lake (3270) (18 acres)

Exit 45 from I-90 leads north and then to rd. 9031, continuing to the Talapus trailhead. It is one of the most heavily visited lakes in Washington, an easy 2 mile walk with a 600' elevation gain. Abundant small eastern brook and stocked rainbow inhabit the lake. There have been occasional reports of cutthroat as well. It was at one time stocked with brown trout to crop the brookies.

Olallie Lake (3780) (13 acres)

Olallie is 1.4 miles beyond Talapus Lake, 500' higher, also reachable from the Pratt Lake trail but a bit farther. There are rainbow successfully spawning in the inlet. Do not fish the inlet and stay out of it, to allow this family of trout to maintain itself. The wild trout here do not appear to grow large, but they are a healthy population exemplary of the capacity of stocked trout to find a way to become self-sustaining.

Pratt Lake (3385) (43 acres)

A very well marked trail leads 5.75 miles from the trailhead, climbing past Olallie Lake and down to Pratt. Its good spawning habitat has historically supplied the lake with rainbow, cutthroat and eastern brook, which are predominant. Mackinaw Trout were stocked at one time as well. **Little Pratt Lake**, (4 acres) has very limited spawning and is occasionally planted.

Lower Tuscohatchie (3420) (32 acres)

Very deep Lower Tuscohatchie is .5 mile east by trail around a ridge beyond Pratt Lake, the lowest of three lakes connected by the outlet stream from Upper

Rainbow Lake

Tuscohatchie. The stream allows the entire system to support wild, self-sustaining rainbow and cutthroat. The lower lake is a total of 6 miles from the Talapus Lake trailhead, a 1600' gain, or 6.3 miles from the Pratt Lake trailhead.

Middle Tuscohatchie Lake

Actually two lakes, the middle lakes are connected by a very short stretch of stream.

Upper Tuscohatchie Lake (4020) (58 acres)

The larger upper lake is about 1.5 miles by way trail from the point where the main trail meets the lower lake. It has a small number of now natural rainbow which have been occasionally supplemented by stocking. There is a small unnamed lake to the west and numerous potholes in the area, some containing trout.

Melakwa Lake (4490) (8 acres)

A very popular 4.5 mile, 2300' gain trail leads to Melakwa and beyond. From Exit 47 off I-90, find the Denny Creek Campground. There is a small road beyond it which crosses the river. There are private homes here, believe it or not. You may have to park at the campground and walk the .3 mile to the trailhead. There is a small lake above Melakwa. This upper lake depends upon stocking to support trout and the lower lake has eastern brook and some reproducing rainbow/cutthroat. As

Windy lake

with any healthy reproducing rainbow or cutthroat population, they should be released but there's no harm in keeping and frying up a brookie or two.

My Lake (3940)

This small lake lies about 1 mile west of Melakwa Lake, cross-country north from the main trail between Melakwa and Lower Tuscohatchie or cross-country from upper Melakwa Lake. An old miner's cabin once existed at this lake. It is reported to have a few naturalized rainbow and is periodically stocked as well.

Windy Lake (4186) (5 acres)

Windy is adjacent to the trail 3 miles beyond Lower Tuscohatchie Lake on the way to Kaleetan Lake. Rainbow are stocked periodically and they do well in this lake.

Kaleetan Lake (3850) (43 acres)

4 miles beyond Lower Tuscohatchie Lake, Kaleetan produces self-sustaining cutthroat and eastern brook.

Ice Lake (4450) (2 acres)

Along with barren Frozen Lake, Ice lies directly east uphill from Kaleetan Lake. There is no established trail. Outlets from both lakes flow into Kaleetan. Ice has been reported to have very limited numbers of reproducing cutthroat.

Scout Lake (3850) (6 acres)

A maze of seemingly ever changing logging roads with gates lead up Hansen Creek toward Scout Lake. It takes approximately 1 mile of brush beating uphill to the lake. Exercise caution here as it gets steep along the way and it is a very heavy devils club area. Scout is periodically stocked and produces small rainbow.

Annette Lake (3640) (18 acres)

Among the most popular hikes in Washington, Annette requires a hike of 3.5 miles, 1700' gain. Find the trailhead off exit 47 to the south side of I-90. The lake features a scenic waterfall. Annette has naturally reproducing cutthroat/rainbow which utilize the lake's outlet, supplemented with rainbow plants. Trout generally average 8-11" with a few larger.

Granite Mt. Lakes

From I-90 take exit 47 back over the freeway west .5 mile to the Granite Mt. trailhead. In approximately 4.5 steep miles on this very popular trail, hikers reach a bench. Anglers carefully scramble from here to reach at least 3 lakes, Denny, Cad and Crystal. The lakes are usually frozen into July, and this trail is well known for avalanches in early summer. Check with a Ranger for conditions. All are reachable from the Tuscohatchie lakes, a longer hike but mostly on established trails.

Denny Lake (4330) (14 acres)

Denny is very deep, surrounded by rock slides and timber, several hundred feet east of Cad

Kaleetan Lake

Lake. About 3.5-4 miles from the trailhead, contour to the lake. It is occasionally stocked with rainbow, supplementing the cutthroat which spawn successfully in this lake's productive habitat.

Cad Lake (4300)

This very small meadow and rock lake provides one of the inlet streams to upper Tuscohatchie Lake. It has been reported to have a few now wild rainbow and eastern brook.

Crystal Lake (4740) (6.5 acres)

Periodically stocked with cutthroat and at one time, golden trout, Crystal is approximately .7 mile west of Denny Lake, due north of the summit of Granite Mt. It drains to upper Tuscohatchie Lake.

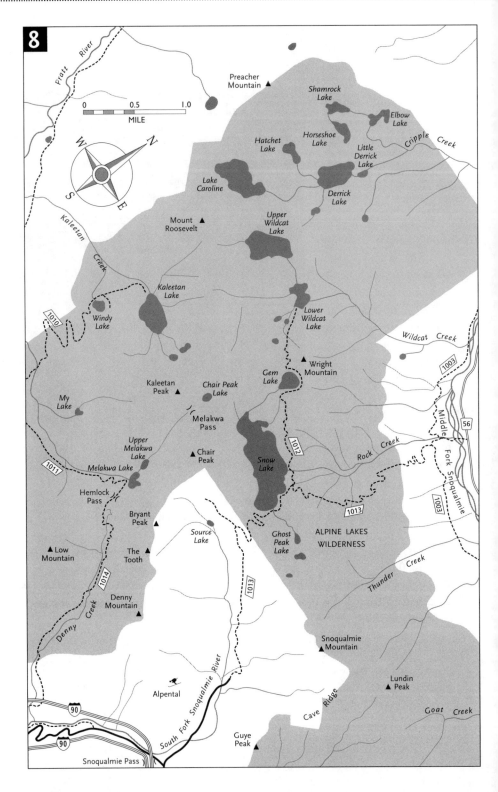

8

Pratt River

Preacher Mountain ▲

Shamrock Lake

Elbow Lake

Cripple Creek

0   0.5   1.0
MILE

Hatchet Lake

Horseshoe Lake

Little Derrick Lake

Lake Caroline

Derrick Lake

Kaleetan Creek

Mount Roosevelt ▲

Upper Wildcat Lake

1010

Kaleetan Lake

Windy Lake

Lower Wildcat Lake

Wildcat Creek

1003

Wright Mountain ▲

Kaleetan Peak ▲

Chair Peak Lake

Gem Lake

Middle Fork Snoqualmie

56

My Lake

Melakwa Pass

1012

Rock Creek

1003

Upper Melakwa Lake

Chair Peak ▲

1011

Melakwa Lake

Snow Lake

1013

Hemlock Pass

Bryant Peak ▲

Source Lake

Ghost Peak Lake

ALPINE LAKES WILDERNESS

Thunder Creek

▲ Low Mountain

1014

The Tooth ▲

Denny Creek

Denny Mountain ▲

1013

Snoqualmie Mountain ▲

Lundin Peak ▲

Alpental

Cave Ridge

Goat Creek

90

South Fork Snoqualmie River

90

Guye Peak ▲

Snoqualmie Pass

SNOQUALMIE PASS

Snow Lake

Alpental Trails   (Map 8)

Take exit 52 off I-90 to the Alpental parking lot and access to some of the most frequently visited high lakes in Washington.

Snow Lake (4016) (159 acres)

Perhaps the most popular hike in the Cascades, the 3 mile Snow Lake trail gains 1300',
the last mile dropping 400' to the lake. Expect to find protected areas along the lake
where overuse has resulted in revegetation work. This large classic mountain lake lies
at the foot of Kaleetan Peak, Chair Peak, and The Tooth. Snow is not a rich lake, rather
unproductive but the lake's rainbow and previously stocked cutthroat apparently
have some limited spawning success and are supplemented by regular stocking, producing mostly small but a few fair size trout. At 1.5 miles in on the trail, a fork leads
left above tiny **Source Lake** (3750) the headwater of the South Fork Snoqualmie River.
It has periodically been stocked with cutthroat but can be fished out early. Release the
trout here to leave other anglers a reasonable chance for some action.

Gem Lake (4851) (15 acres)

Gem is a beautiful lake on the south side of Wright Mt. 2 miles by trail beyond and
900' higher than Snow Lake, a 5 mile hike in all. It apparently does not have a self-sus-

Upper Wildcat Lake

taining population of trout, is not stocked and may be barren. Despite this, there are old reports of good fishing.

Lower Wildcat Lake (3920) (19 acres)
A cutthroat stocked lake 1.5 miles past Gem Lake by trail and 600' below, Lower Wildcat Lake is 6.5 miles from the Alpental parking lot. **Upper Wildcat (4218) (45 acres)** is west uphill .3 by a sketchy trail, its outlet stream feeding the lower lake. Cutthroat spawn successfully in limited numbers in this stream. The lake is also periodically stocked with rainbow and produces good size trout. Both lakes are located in rugged, scenic environs. Two small potholes feed the lower lake and have held fish at times.

Lake Caroline (4740) (60 acres)
To the west of the Wildcat Lakes, Caroline lies on the north side of Mt. Roosevelt and Hatchet Lake east of Preacher Mt., and drains to Derrick Lake. It is about a mile cross-country from Upper Wildcat Lake, also uphill sharply from the Pratt River Trail. This is remote country even though close to Snoqualmie Pass. Caroline is occasionally stocked with trout.

Derrick Lake (3686) (37 acres)
Quite remote, Derrick lies a very difficult mile cross-country north-northwest from Upper Wildcat Lake. It is reported to have now wild rainbow/cutthroat and possi-

Lake Caroline

bly golden trout. Catch and release should be employed at Derrick. **Little Derrick Lake** (3650) (2 acres) is 500' from Derrick, fed by its outlet stream.

Hatchet Lake (4026) (7 acres)

This secluded lake is the headwater of the southwest inlet stream of Derrick Lake, on the south side of Preacher Mt. Far from any trail, travel west over a ridge from Upper Wildcat Lake or up the Hatchet Lake outlet from Derrick Lake. It has a naturally reproducing population of cutthroat and is reported to have golden trout. It is occasionally stocked as well.

Shamrock Lakes

Elbow (3900) (6 acres), **Horseshoe** (4300) (8 acres) and **Cathedral Lake** (4000) (8 acres) are 3 very beautiful lakes lying northwest of Derrick Lake and draining to Cripple Creek, three long miles from the end of any trail. Cathedral and Elbow have naturally reproducing cutthroat/rainbow, Horseshoe depends upon stocking and has occasionally been stocked with golden trout. Anglers report good fishing in all three lakes. These lakes can be reached cross-country from the Wildcat Lakes or by an obscure route via Preacher Mountain from the Middle Fork Snoqualmie River trail, beginning about 2 miles downstream from the Dingford Creek bridge.

Pacific Crest Trail from Snoqualmie Pass

The Pacific Crest Trail crosses Snoqualmie Pass at I-90 and is the main hiking highway, running primarily north/south through Washington's Central Cascades. A great hiking/fishing trip is taken every summer by hikers, trekking from Stevens Pass to Snoqualmie Pass, or reversing the route, approximately 70 miles in all. Expect to find lots of company in places, few people in others. There are unlimited opportunities for side trips to more secluded lakes.

Gravel Lake (5100) (9 acres)

The Crest Trail passes between Ridge Lake and Gravel Lake at 7.3 miles from Snoqualmie Pass. This alpine lake is 200' downhill to the north from the trail. However, at approximately 5 miles in on the Crest Trail, the famous Kendall Catwalk is encountered. Unless it is bare, turn around and make a day hike out of your trip because it's too dangerous to cross when there is snow on it. The lake has limited numbers of naturalized cutthroat and is occasionally supplemented with rainbow and golden trout.

Ridge Lake (5220) (2 acres)

The Crest Trail passes this small lake 7.3 miles from Snoqualmie Pass. Its outlet flows into Alaska Lake. It is periodically stocked with rainbow.

Edds Lake (4300) (26 acres)

Two miles beyond Ridge Lake, the Crest Trail passes Edds Lake to the northwest, 800' very steeply below. It is also accessible from Joe Lake, up and over the ridge between the two lakes. Once known for its large cutthroat, it gets regular plants of golden trout with some natural reproduction as well.

Lodge Lake (3125) (9 acres)

An easy two mile hike leaves from Snoqualmie Ski Area, travels across fireweed-covered slopes and heads behind a ridge, passing shallow Beaver Lake on the way. If you can stand the noise from I-90, this is a nice simple hike to a lake which is a steady producer of stocked rainbow trout, along with a few naturally reproducing cutthroat, which should be released. It is tough lake to fish from shore.

Hyak Area Lakes (Map 9)

There are 5 lakes next to or close by a complicated road system from Hyak Ski Resort, north of the ski lifts. Exit 54 off I-90, leads to the lakes. Check on the condition and access up the road. You may have to park and walk up the road to the lakes. Depending upon road conditions, the lakes can get very heavy fishing pressure.

Hyak Lake (3500) (2 acres)

One mile before its end, the road passes within .25 mile of this shallow lake, which is frequently fished. It is the headwater of Hyak Creek and is periodically stocked.

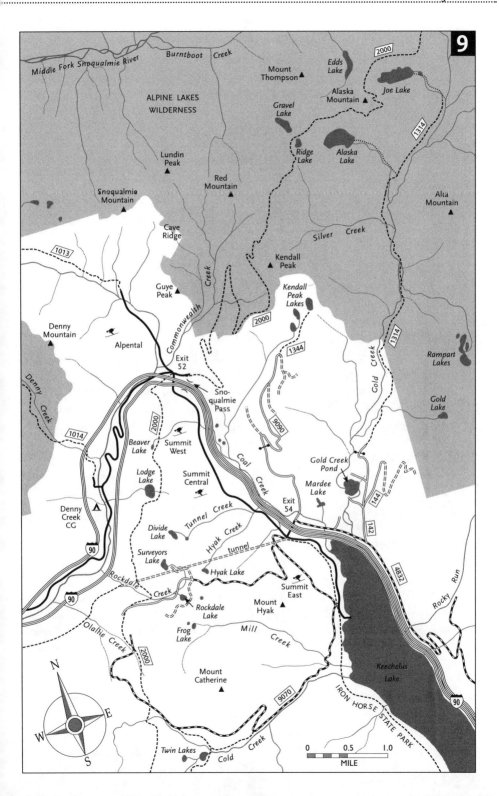

Rockdale Lake (3540) (2 acres)

Follow the road past Hyak Lake, soon passing by Rockdale to the left. Regularly stocked rainbow supplement a few naturally reproducing rainbow in the lake.

Frog Lake (3500)

A very small boggy pond at the head of Mill Creek lies about .4 mile south of Rockdale cross-country through brushy territory. It was at one time stocked with eastern brook.

Surveyor's Lake (3980) (5 acres)

Follow the road about .5 mile beyond Hyak Lake to find Surveyors, approximately .5 mile north of Hyak Lake. It has historically been stocked with rainbow, and produces generally small trout.

Divide Lake (3870) (2 acres)

The headwater of Tunnel Creek, Divide is approximately .3 mile north of Surveyor's Lake. It is consistently planted with rainbow.

Twin Lakes (3090) (4 acres and 2 acres)

Take rd. 9070 from Hyak to the trailhead and a 1 mile hike to Lower Twin Lake. These two lakes are inhabited by very active beavers, which have built dams here and there. The smaller lake is above about .5 mile and a mean bushwhack to find. There are small, naturally reproducing cutthroat in the lower lake and some have been reported in the upper lake. Both are periodically planted with rainbow.

Gold Creek Area (Map 8, 9)

From I-90 take the Hyak exit and drive north. There are plenty of signs to Gold Creek. It is the gateway to several lakes quite close to the Seattle/Eastside area. Gold Creek and Gold Creek Pond may be closed to fishing to protect bull trout.

Kendall Peak Lakes (4300) and (4740)

The three Kendall Peak Lakes require a 2.5 mile walk from a gate on an old logging road, beginning about .5 mile from I-90. Walk the road, passing road forks, to an old trailhead at the end of the road, leading another 1 mile and 300' up to the lowest lake. A mountain bike makes this a faster trip. The lowest lake is swampy and can be tough fishing. The middle lake is in open timber and the upper lake is a beautiful mountain cirque. These lakes were heavily visited and fished before the road was gated and are recovering well. They are regularly planted with rainbow.

Alaska Lake (4230) (35 acres)

The Rocky Run Rd. leads to a left on rd.144 near the Gold Creek Pond Picnic area. Rd. 142 travels about 1.5 miles to the trailhead. Hike approximately a mile on the gated road, pass the gate to the trail, leading 4 flat but confusing miles up Gold

Joe Lake

Creek, avoiding lots of side trails, with a couple of fords along the way. Then find a way trail to Alaska Lake, a very steep, brushy, rocky one mile and 1100′ foot gain. The trail is unmaintained but there are often trail markers along the way. The Crest Trail also travels past this lake, but it is a nearly 1000′ dangerous descent below the trail and a long 7.5 miles to this point from the trailhead. The lake lies amid meadows, cliffs, rock slides and heather. It is a cutthroat lake.

Joe Lake (4624) (30 acres)

Continue on Gold Creek trail 1.7 miles, gaining 1500′ beyond the side trail leading to Alaska Lake, 5.7 total miles from the trailhead on a very rough trail at times. The trail climbs 1000′ in its last mile. There are mini-icebergs in this cutthroat lake clear into late summer.

Keechelus Lake Area (Map 9, 10)

Lake Keechelus is a 6 mile long artificial lake, the source of the Yakima River. I-90 runs alongside it and there is a seasonal boat launch on the southwest side of the lake. A boat is necessary to effectively fish the lake. It contains kokanee, cutthroat, rainbow, eastern brook, bull trout, which must be released, squawfish and the freshwater ling cod, burbot. Its best fishing is often in front of the dam or near the inlet. The main attraction for anglers has historically been an expanded catch limit for Kokanee, which average 10-12″, along with some nice cutthroat. Several alpine

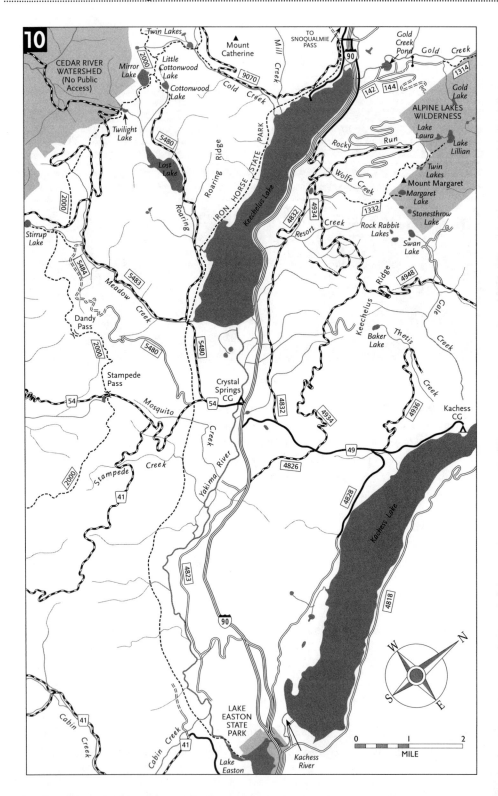

10

CEDAR RIVER WATERSHED (No Public Access)

Twin Lakes

Mount Catherine

TO SNOQUALMIE PASS

Gold Creek Pond

Gold Creek

2000

Mirror Lake

Little Cottonwood Lake

9070

Cold Creek

90

142 144

1314

Cottonwood Lake

Gold Lake

Twilight Lake

5480

Roaring Ridge

IRON HORSE STATE PARK

Keechelus Lake

Rocky Run

Lake Laura

ALPINE LAKES WILDERNESS

Lake Lillian

Lost Lake

Roaring

Wolfe Creek

Twin Lakes

Mount Margaret

Margaret Lake

2000

4832

4934

Resort

Creek

Stonesthrow Lake

Stirrup Lake

Rock Rabbit Lakes

Swan Lake

5484

Meadow Creek

5483

Ridge

4948

Cole

Dandy Pass

2000

5480

5480

Baker Lake

Thetis

Creek

Keechelus

Stampede Pass

Crystal Springs CG

Creek

4832

4924

4936

Kachess CG

54

Mosquito

54

49

4826

Yakima River

Stampede Creek

Creek

41

2000

4828

Kachess Lake

4823

90

4818

Lake Easton State Park

Cabin Creek

41

Cabin Creek

41

Lake Easton

Kachess River

N
W E
S

0   1   2
MILE

lakes are nearby. Brushy **Meadow Creek** flows into the south end of the Lake and contains cutthroat, rainbow, whitefish and even burbot.

Margaret Lake (4790) (4 acres)

Find the frontage road on the north side of I-90 from Exit 54. Follow it as it goes uphill, redesignated rd. 4832, then on rd. 4934, until reaching a parking lot often full of cars. Anglers know that a trip to this lake and a little bushwhacking in the nearby area can result in a nice fishing trip. A formal trail leads to the lake, at the base of grassy Mt. Margaret, 3 miles, part of which is an old road, not especially scenic, the noise of I-90 below, the rest a trail up and over a ridge, then down 400' to the lake. Margaret contains cutthroat or rainbow, depending upon stocking policy.

Within short but dense cross-country walking are **Stonesthrow Lake (4410) (2 acres)** a rainbow stocked meadow lake which may also have some limited natural cutthroat reproduction; **Swan Lake (4040) (7 acres)**, periodically stocked with cutthroat; and **Rock Rabbit Lakes**, both of which receive regular rainbow plants, at the head of Swan Lake's south inlet stream. Rock Rabbit Lakes may be subject to winter-kill. These three lakes have in the past been much more easily reached from a series of logging roads by continuing beyond the trailhead to Margaret on rd. 4934, then left on 4948, and left again on an old road just after passing Gale Creek. Check with USFS to be sure these roads are open. They are deteriorating and may be closed. The lakes are all regularly stocked. Stonesthrow requires the most searching to find.

Lake Lillian (4800) (17 acres)

Regularly stocked with rainbow, Lillian is a scenic and popular lake, but a rather arduous day trip, 4.5 miles. Hike 2.5 miles up to the ridge, passing the side trail to Margaret Lake, continue along the ridge, then drop 600,' to **Twin Lakes (4600)**, two very small, shallow ponds, both of which are planted with rainbow and also probably have reproducing trout, then down a bit more, and up some more, to Lillian. Lillian's outlet stream feeds rainbow stocked **Lake Laura (4410) (4 acres)** .2 mile south and a few hundred feet below. Knowledgeable cross-country hikers reach Laura and Lillian from Rocky Run Rd. by another route.

Gold Lake (5000) (8 acres)

Gold Lake is regularly stocked with rainbow. It lies in a pocket on the west side of Rampart Ridge, northwest about a mile from Lillian. There is no formal trail to the lake.

Baker Lake (4220) (5 acres)

Baker is also known as Thetis Lake because it heads up Thetis Creek. A logging road follows the creek from the west shore of Lake Kachess to within 1 mile of the lake. Bushwhack from here. Or take a road to the right off rd. 4948, which comes closer, but there is no stream to follow. Baker contains eastern brook.

Cottonwood Lake

Upper Yakima River

There are some pleasant surprises in store for anglers willing to work hard at bushwhacking and thrashing through the trees to search out the upper Yakima River between Lake Keechelus and Lake Easton. It contains rainbow, eastern brook and west slope cutthroat. Bull trout may also be encountered and must be released. Until the Keechelus Dam flows are reduced late in the summer, often not until September, it is generally too high, difficult to fish and just not worth the effort. Some diehards do claim to float it and fish successfully with nymphs when it is high. Once it is at low flow and stabilized, it has fair to good fishing for small to medium size trout, with a few more sizable rainbow found in its deepest holes.

This section of the Yakima has some very long, deep holes and runs and decent riffles, but a lot of walking is necessary to get to the good spots. There is access here and there from I-90, particularly from the Cabin Creek Rd. exit but several miles of river are a considerable bushwhack from any road. The upper Yakima does not have large numbers of fish and is under barbless hook, no bait regulations. It is strongly recommended that all fish be released. Anglers seeking bigger trout and better habitat find it worthwhile to travel a bit farther east, to the catch and release section of the Yakima downstream from Lake Easton and in the Cle Elum area.

Stirrup Lake (3550) (9 acres)

This heavily visited lake holds eastern brook and is regularly stocked with rainbow. The hike is short enough for very small children and provides a chance to catch a youngster's first mountain trout. Take exit 62 from I-90 to the west side, then rd. 54, to rd.5480, then left on rd. 5483, passing a right on rd. 5484, shortly left on the Meadow Pass Rd. winding uphill to the pass and the trail to the lake. There is also a trail of about 1.5 miles uphill from rd.5484.

Lost Lake (3100) (145 acres)

Adjacent to rd. 5480 about a mile west of Keechelus Lake, this Lost Lake contains kokanee and brook trout. Although brookies average only 9 inches, there are some lunkers.

There is a boat launch, as this lake is very large and boat fishing is most popular.

Cottonwood Lake (3940) (8 acres)

By continuing past Lost Lake on rd. 5480, bearing right at the first fork, the trailhead to Cottonwood and Mirror Lake is found. The road is in tough shape at the end and a little extra walking may be required. The trail reaches Cottonwood in .5 mile. The short hike makes this a good place to fish from a float tube. The lake contains healthy non-stunted brook trout and stocked rainbow. It gets a lot of pressure, which may account for the good size of the brookies and catch and release is appropriate here. By the end of summer, only the lucky or wary trout are left. The shoreline is degraded and deserves special care.

Mirror Lake

Little Cottonwood Lake (4040)

Basically a large pond, Little Cottonwood is found by hiking past Cottonwood approximately .5 mile to the junction with the Pacific Crest Trail, turning right and soon passing the pond off to the right. It is quite shallow and has contained trout from time to time. It has periodically been stocked with rainbow.

Mirror Lake (4195) (29 acres)

An easy 1 mile walk from the Cottonwood Lake trailhead, Mirror is a classic mountain lake with deep, crystal water and lovely surroundings, at the base of Tinkham Peak. It has a nice campsite but expect lots of visitors. It has historically contained brookies and produces rainbow with an occasional lunker but is tough to fish except from a raft or float tube.

Twilight Lake (3600) (2 acres)

About one mile farther on the Crest Trail south of Mirror Lake, Twilight gets occasional plants of cutthroat.

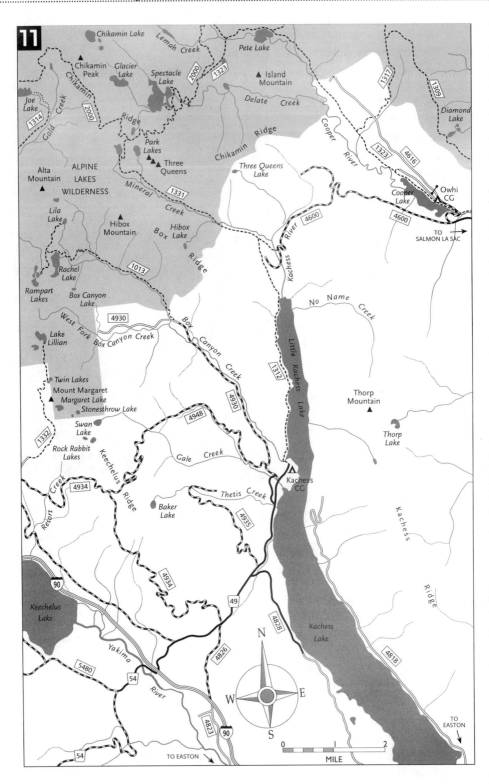

11

Chikamin Lake
Lemah Creek
Pete Lake
Chikamin Peak
Glacier Lake
Spectacle Lake
▲ Island Mountain
2000
1323
1517
1309
Joe Lake
1314
Chikamin
Gold Creek
2000
Ridge
Delate Creek
Cooper River
Diamond Lake
Park Lakes
Three Queens
Chikamin
Three Queens Lake
1323
4616
Alta Mountain ▲
ALPINE LAKES WILDERNESS
Mineral
1331
Ridge
Cooper Lake
Owhi CG
Lila Lake
Hibox Mountain
Hibox Lake
Box Ridge
Kachess River
4600
4600
TO SALMON LA SAC
Rachel Lake
1013
Rampart Lakes
Box Canyon Lake
West Fork Box Canyon Creek
4930
Box Canyon Creek
No Name Creek
Lake Lillian
1312
Little Kachess Lake
Thorp Mountain ▲
Twin Lakes
Mount Margaret ▲ Margaret Lake
Stonesthrow Lake
4948
4930
Thorp Lake
1332
Swan Lake
Rock Rabbit Lakes
Keechelus Ridge
Gale Creek
Kachess CG
Kachess
Creek
4934
Resort
Baker Lake
Thetis Creek
4935
Ridge
90
4934
Keechelus Lake
49
4838
Kachess Lake
5480
Yakima
4826
4818
54
River
N
W E
S
TO EASTON
4823
90
0   1   2
MILE
54
TO EASTON

Kachess Lake Area   (Map 10, 11)
Kachess River

The very short lower Kachess river runs from the Kachess Dam under I-90 to Lake Easton and contains a variety of fish. Access is very difficult but aggressive waders can locate fish in holding areas. It runs full most of the season and is difficult to fish but there have been reports of good sized trout moving into the river from Lake Easton at times. The river can be reached from Sparks Rd. off I-90. It is a no-bait, barbless hook stream. All bull trout must be released. Above Lake Kachess, it is closed upstream to its junction with Mineral Creek. Mineral Creek is closed to fishing upstream to the Wilderness Boundary.

Kachess Lake (2245) (4540 acres)

Kachess, a very popular, 13 mile long reservoir with good camping areas and boat launches, produces 9-11" kokanee by early June. Rainbow, cutthroat and burbot are also taken. There is a 16-fish catch limit for kokanee. It also contains bull trout, which must be released. Anglers who learn how to fish the lake have success but most do not do well. Many use deep trolling methods from boats equipped with motors. Those who learn where and when to find schools of fish can use other methods successfully. Kachess is just north of I-90, accessible by two freeway exits. The narrow northern arm of Kachess is called little Kachess and provides the best fishing.

A number of small tributaries to Lake Kachess contain small cutthroat, rainbow and eastern brook, with a few to 9-12." These include **Gale Creek**, **Thetis Creek**, and **Box Canyon Creek**. All except Box Canyon Creek are difficult to fish in their lower reaches, which may be closed to protect bull trout, but on the terrain above Lake Kachess they level off in places, particularly above major falls, where there are low gradient reaches with good numbers of small trout available to those willing to bushwhack. Box Canyon Creek is a large creek and has excellent trout habitat for several miles. It is presently closed, to protect bull trout, upstream from its mouth to the rd. 4930 bridge, approximately 4 miles. From the bridge, there is about 1 mile of good fishing water, up to the Rachel Lake trailhead. Look for beautiful small west slope cutthroat in this stream. Catch and release is imperative when fishing here.

Lake Easton (2100) (237 acres)

Located just west of the town of Easton, this reservoir lake has fair fishing after late May for 8-10" rainbow.

Cabin Creek

Cabin Creek contains cutthroat, rainbow and a few brookies. The lower stretch of Cabin Creek contains few fish but some of the ponds on the creek farther upstream were stocked with eastern brook many years ago and are worth the effort to find and fish. Cabin Creek is accessible from Easton on Cabin Creek Rd. but cannot be reached from the Cabin Creek Rd. exit off 1-90.

Easton Ponds

Three small ponds were created near the town of Easton during the construction of I-90. They are regularly planted with rainbow and can provide some good action early in the season. They are adjacent to the freeway on the north side and noise is a serious distraction. They are used in Spring for a short time as a coho acclimation pond and are closed early April-May.

Box Canyon Trail Area   (Map 11)

An extremely popular but moderately difficult trail leads from Box Canyon Rd., off I-90 at exit 62. Take the road to Kachess Lake Campground, then to Box Canyon Rd., rd. 4930, 4 miles, finally left and shortly into a usually packed parking lot.

Box Canyon Lake (4500) (2 acres)

At about 2.75 easy miles in on the Box Canyon/Rachel Lake trail, the outlet stream from Rachel is joined by Box Canyon's outlet stream, flowing in on the left of the trail. This shallow lake lies .5 mile southeast of Rachel Lake and the best access is cross-country from the southeast tip of Rachel. Some have bushwhacked 1300' up the right side of the outlet stream to reach the lake. It it periodically stocked and can produce cutthroat to 14- 15", with most trout 8-12".

Rachel Lake (4600) (27 acres)

This very popular, beautiful park-like lake lying high on Rampart Ridge is reached by 3 miles of deceptively easy hiking, leading to a one mile, very steep 1300' gain, to the lake, a total of 4 miles. It is periodically stocked with cutthroat. Most cutts are 7-9" with a few larger.

Rampart Lakes (5100) (0.5 and 7 acres)

Continue beyond Rachel Lake by turning right for .5 mile, rather steep at the end, then turn left as the trail Ts, hiking an up/down mile to two Rampart Lakes. They are situated in an area of great scenery and several lakes, but are very popular and heavily frequented. There are at least 4 lakes and dozens of glacier carved ponds set in granite. The lakes are 5.5 miles from the trailhead, 2400' gain, and contain stocked cutthroat, mostly small to medium size.

Lila Lake (5200) (3 acres)

At the T beyond Rachel Lake, head right one mile to Lila. It has two adjacent ponds. Although it tends to freeze solid in the winter, it is occasionally stocked with rainbow. The ponds above Lila Lake are thought to be devoid of fish.

EAST OF SNOQUALMIE PASS

Spectacle Lake

Mineral Creek Trail   (Map 12)

Mineral Creek trailhead is found by driving to Cooper Lake, passing it on the south, then 2.1 miles through Cooper Pass, finally bearing right 2.5 miles to the trailhead. The trail, tr.1331, is often very brushy with lots of downed timber and can be rough going.

Three Queens Lake (5400) (1.5 acres)

About .5 mile up Mineral Creek trail, Three Queens Lake lies to the north at the base of Three Queens Mountain. It appears boxed in and extremely difficult to reach. Only the intrepid get here. Some say the best route is from Mineral Creek Mine cabin. It is on the tail end of Chikamin Ridge in a seldom-traveled area, the headwater of the last stream entering the Kachess River before its confluence with Mineral Creek. Stocking records show that it is a golden trout lake, but it is small enough that it may experience winter-kill.

Hi Box Lake (5000) (3 acres)

Hi Box is a small but deep, lovely lake located on the top of Wild Box Ridge. Take the Mineral Creek trail 2 miles until a small stream drains into Mineral Creek from the south. The lake is situated up the creek 1.5 very steep, difficult miles. Frozen until later in the summer, it has occasionally been stocked with rainbow and may have potential spawning habitat.

Park Lakes

The Mineral Creek trail reaches Upper Park Lake (4700) (11 acres) at 4.5 miles, a 2300′ elevation gain from the trailhead. Lower Park Lake (4500) (9 acres) is .25 mile to the east in a bowl. Great views are available by continuing on the trail to the junction with the Pacific Crest Trail and beyond. Both lakes have received regular rainbow plants.

Spectacle Lake (4350) (81 acres)

Just beyond Park Lakes, the trail meets the Pacific Crest Trail. Turn right and at 3 miles, head left for .5 mile to the lake. The lake is also reachable from Pete Lake in about the same total hiking distance. There are eastern brook in this easy to fish lake. It is also regularly stocked with cutthroat.

Glacier Lake (5300) (21 acres)

High above Spectacle Lake at the foot of some dazzling scenery, Glacier's outlet flows into Spectacle on its southwest shore. There are remnants of an old trail but reaching the lake requires route-finding and bushwhacking. There is an unnamed lake at 5700′ buried in the rocks above Glacier Lake and several other unnamed lakes at 6900′ at the foot of Chimney Rock, surrounded by ice. The lake is also accessible cross-country from the PCT above Park Lakes via Mineral Creek trail. It has long been periodically stocked with golden trout.

Cross-country Hiking to Central Cascades High Lake

Chikamin Lake (5800) (17 acres)

Above the head of Spectacle Lake's northern inlet, Chikamin is a true beauty spot seldom visited. There is no trail and no completely safe way to reach it. Its outlet has a series of waterfalls. It was at one time stocked with cutthroat, which have naturalized and successfully reproduce. A nearby pothole has also been reported to hold fish.

Cle Elum River Area
(Map 11,12, 13)
Lower Cle Elum River

This is a very popular recreational area, with numerous campgrounds along the river and at Salmon-La-Sac. Fishing is surprisingly tough in this large river, both from the dam at Cle Elum Lake downstream to the river's junction with the Yakima River and above the lake up through Salmon La Sac. The river looks perfect, snorkel surveys have found good numbers of cutthroat and rainbow along

Cle Elum River downstream from Salmon La Sac

with whitefish, brookies and even burbot in deep holes along the river but for some reason anglers catch few trout. It is possible that the granitic nature of the area through which the Cle Elum flows allows for only a limited food supply for trout.

In general, bushwhacking to places not usually fished is necessary to have a fair day's fishing, especially above the lake to Salmon La Sac where it is fished incessantly during the summer. Once the river drops to its low in August and September, trout to 12" can be found at the head of the larger pools, but those pools are few and quite a distance from each other. Catch and release is the best practice on the river. There is selective rule fishing from the dam downstream, but bait is allowed upstream. WDFW may wish to designate a stretch of the river above the lake for selective fishing or catch and release to see if this river can support a higher quality trout fishery.

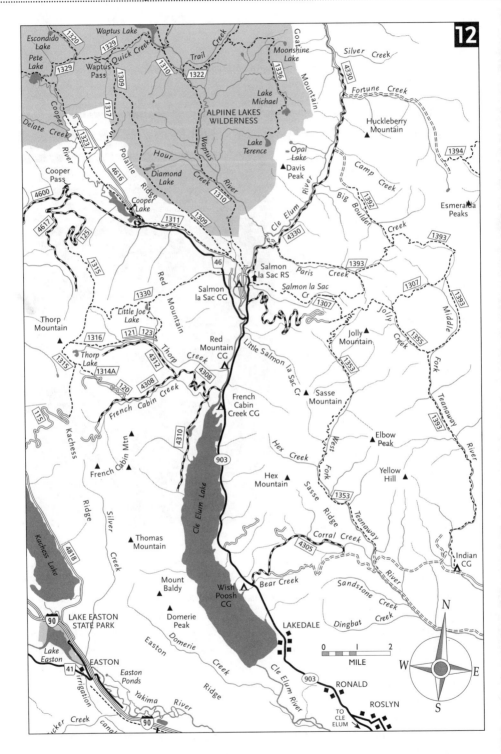

Any reliable dry fly such as an Elk Hair Caddis, Parachute Adams or Wulf will work just fine if the fish are in the mood to rise. Otherwise, use a standard nymph or streamer.

Cle Elum Lake (2223) (4,810 acres)

This large storage reservoir near the town of Cle Elum gets light fishing pressure, and is a fair producer of kokanee. It has rainbow cutthroat, brook, whitefish, suckers, shiners, and bull trout as well. Bull trout must be released. Trolling is most effective. Some Lake Trout, Mackinaw, are taken each spring, and burbot are also available. A very few mackinaw in the 20 lb. range have been reported. Fly anglers have the best luck fishing deep, near the inlet and lucking into the occasional hatch on one of those rare, still evenings. Some of the tributaries contain small trout, including French Cabin Creek and Thorp Creek.

Thorp Lake (4670) (10 acres)

Turn off I-90 at exit 80 to Roslyn. From Roslyn, 11 miles takes you to the end of Lake Cle Elum and shortly to rd. 4308. Turn left and drive 3.2 miles, then right on rd. 4312 for 1.3 miles to the trailhead to this popular lake. A gated road leads from this point across Thorp Creek, shortly to a junction. Take this to the left, then within .25 mile the trail takes off uphill. At 2.75 miles is a trail intersection almost at the lake, turn left and find the lake within a few hundred yards. Elevation gain is 1200'. People in a bigger hurry with big vehicles, continue up rd. 4312 to its end, then contour west across Thorp Creek to the trail or simply bushwhack from the road end to the lake. It is regularly stocked with rainbow.

Little Joe Lake (4690) (5 acres)

Follow the directions to Thorp Lake but instead of turning left at the first junction past the gated road, continue on, cross a creek and look for the trail to the lake, off to the left. The rainbow stocked lake is 1.75 miles from here, a steep 1100' and the trail is obscure in spots but as long as you can hear the creek, you will make it. This is not a hike to take for pleasure. At one time, Little Joe was more easily reached off a logging road southwest from Cooper Lake.

Cooper River

The Cooper River has rainbow, cutthroat, eastern brook and brown trout. It is one of the few rivers in Washington containing all four species and one can, if very lucky, tempt all four to a fly or lure in one day. It also contains bull trout, which must be released. Catch and release is recommended for all species in this river, as the trout are not abundant.

There is easy access to the lower section of this medium size river both from rd. 46 above Cle Elum Lake to Cooper Lake and from a trail along most of the length of the lower river, allowing access here and there for fishing for mostly small trout. This trail runs from Salmon La Sac Campground upstream to Cooper Lake. Later in

The size of stocked Central Cascades Cutthroat can surprise anglers.

the summer, a few larger trout drop downstream into the river from Cooper Lake and can be found within a short distance below the lake, along with smaller trout. Higher concentrations and larger fish have been found in the flat stretches above Salmon La Sac, where the Cooper flows through the campground. It is pounded in the campground and upstream a ways, so some upstream wading is necessary to get to infrequently fished spots. Some nice fish, rainbow to 12"and a bit larger, await anglers willing to work to find the right spots. Many people hike the trail from Salmon La Sac to Cooper Lake but few take the time to fish except at both ends of the trail.

The upper river runs from Pete Lake to Cooper Lake, accessible by a 5 mile trail, allowing for lots of river access. It is not heavily fished and can provide some nice surprises to anglers willing to explore. A snorkel survey found a 26" brown trout not far above Cooper Lake. The water is crystal clear and the pools are good walks apart, making for difficult fishing, but the river's challenges may be worth the effort. Sight fishing for large brown trout may be a possibility, given the survey results.

Cooper Lake (2788) (120 acres)

Cooper is about one mile long and has brook trout, rainbow, cutthroat, kokanee and brown trout. It is regularly stocked. Gasoline motors are prohibited. Veteran fly and spin anglers like to fish the upper end of the lake, where the Cooper River flows in. A boat or float tube is necessary for good fishing. Some sizable browns are taken every year, with fish to 17-20" showing up occasionally. Cooper Lake is accessible by rd.46

from rd.903 above Cle Elum Lake. A road parallels the eastern shore and there are places here and there to fish from shore or launch a boat or float tube.

Pete Lake (2980) (37 acres)

Drive to Cooper Lake, taking the lower road around the right side of the lake to its end. The trail, 5.5 miles on a flat grade along the Cooper River, makes for a popular day hike and horse trail, and one can fish the upper Cooper River as well. Pete is an eastern brook lake, occasionally stocked with rainbow.

Lemah Lake (3900)

Lemah is essentially a swampy area at the head of Lemah

Escondido Lake

Creek, a tributary to Pete Lake. There is no trail from Pete Lake. There are unnamed ponds nearby north of Delate Meadows. It is unknown whether Lemah or the ponds hold trout.

Escondido Lake (4630) (4 acres)

From Pete Lake, tr. 1329 heads uphill to the right, gaining elevation for 1.7 miles to a junction with tr.1320 and 1.8 more miles on a neglected trail to this alpine lake, set in lovely country, 9 miles from the trailhead at Cooper Lake. It is believed to have a fair population of naturally reproducing cutthroat and some large trout have been caught here in the past.

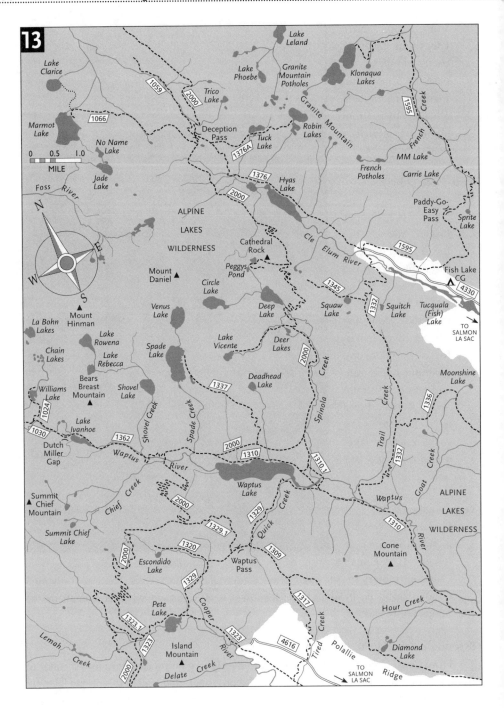

Salmon La Sac Area   (Map 12,13)

Ever-popular Salmon La Sac Campground is the starting point for some good hike-in stream and lake fishing.

Diamond Lake (4950) (5 acres)

From the trailhead at Salmon La Sac Campground, the main trail leads .7 to a fork. Take the right fork, tr. 1309 another approximately 5 miles to the lake and its two close by ponds. A 2500' gain, this is a pleasant trail to a small alpine lake, sometimes reported to have good fishing, with an occasional lunker. It is regularly stocked with cutthroat.

Lower Waptus River

From Salmon La Sac, the Waptus River trail travels two relatively easy miles to access to the Waptus River. Fish upstream or downstream from here and you will have little company. The trail continues close to or next to the river for another 6 miles on its way up to Waptus Lake. The Waptus, a sizable river with red rock and greenish water has good fishing for small, beautiful mountain stream trout with a scattered few in the more sizable class. There are rainbow, cutthroat, brook and possibly bull trout in the lower section with predominately rainbow closer to the lake. A few visits up the trail to the Waptus, finding the best water, will surely make you want to return. July is generally a bit too early, but August through mid- September is prime time for this hiking/fishing jaunt.

There is also easy access to the lower Waptus at its confluence with the Cle Elum River. Above Salmon La Sac, rd. 134 leads to the left downhill to the Davis Peak trail. Follow the trail down to the bridge which crosses the Cle Elum River to where the Waptus flows in. One can fish up the Waptus, quite large in this reach, for several miles, with some minor rock climbing and bushwhacking in places. While it gets heavily fished in the first few hundred yards, it has very nice habitat upstream and contains a few small brookies and cutthroat, but mostly rainbow, with a few to 12" and possibly larger, since there are some very deep holes in this section of the river. It is also reported to contain a few brown trout.

For dry fly fishing, try the usual favorites, Elk Hair Caddis, Royal Wulf and Parachute Adams, size 10-14, with a size 12 your best bet. Nymph fishing works well, using a bead head Hare's Ear or other popular nymph as a dropper below a large dry fly or terrestrial, especially a Hopper pattern later in the Summer.

Moonshine Lake (5400)

Tiny Moonshine Lake is found cross-country east of tr.1336, about 1.5 miles from its junction with tr.1322, which in turn heads east from the Waptus Lake trail. In all, it's about an 11 mile hike from Salmon La Sac, or 6 miles from Tucquala Meadow. It is reported to hold rainbow.

Waptus Lake

Lake Michael (5100) (17 acres)

By continuing on tr.1336, a total of about 8.7 miles from Tucquala Meadow and 13.5 from Salmon La Sac, hikers reach Michael, which produces good sized rainbow and is regularly stocked.

Lake Terence (5600) (14 acres)

Terence is 2 splendid hiking miles beyond Lake Michael, very isolated though only one mile above the Cle Elum River Rd. It contains stocked rainbow.

Waptus Lake (2980) (246 acres)

Two mile long Waptus Lake serves as the Grand Central Station of hiking trails in the area, and is the base camp for visiting several nearby lakes. It is 8.5 miles from Salmon La Sac on a relatively flat grade, with plenty of access to Waptus River fishing along the way. The lake has eastern brook, rainbow, cutthroat and bull trout, which must be released. Some big fish inhabit this natural lake, to 22" and occasionally larger but it is challenging to catch fish. A raft or float tube is very helpful.

Upper Waptus River

The river above Waptus Lake flows through a long flat and is accessible from the trails above the lake for much of its length, though bushbeating is often necessary. It is reported to contain cutthroat, some eastern brook and rainbow and cuttbows as well. It is seldom fished and curious anglers willing to fish a day or two might make some interesting discoveries.

Lake Ivanhoe (4700) (21 acres)

Ivanhoe is a long 15 trail miles from Salmon La Sac. Hike 6.5 miles beyond Waptus Lake, the first 3.5 along the lake and the Waptus Valley, then uphill another 3 miles to the lake, switchbacking steeply in places. Small naturally repro-ducing cutthroat to 9" are plentiful. The lake sits at the foot of Dutch Miller Gap and there are several unnamed lakes above it at 5500'. This hiking route allows anglers to continue on, making a long trip from the Cle Elum side of the Cascades to the Middle Fork Snoqualmie Valley on the west side.

Lake Ivanhoe

Summit Chief Lake (5500) (5 acres)

Planted with golden trout, Summit Chief lies at the head of Chief Creek, a tributary to the Upper Waptus River. There is no trail. North/northeast one mile of Summit Chief Lake there is a small unnamed lake at 5499' and even higher, above this lake is anoth-er unnamed lake at 6500' lying amidst glaciers at the foot of Middle Chief Mt.

Shovel Lake (4000) (27 acres)

This lonely mountain lake lies west over a rugged ridge from Spade Lake. From Waptus Lake, take the Crest trail 2 miles, crossing Shovel Creek, then bushwhack 2 miles up the outlet to the lake. It has good spawning habitat and has been known to produce cutthroat to 16." Trout 8-11" are abundant.

Lake Rebecca (4750) (13 acres)

This lake is found 2 miles up the west fork of its outlet to the Shovel Lake inlet, no trail. Stocked cutthroat have taken hold in this lake and are now naturally reproducing,

Spade Lake

resulting in ample numbers of small trout.

Lake Rowena (5100) (25 acres)
Very beautiful Rowena lies .3 mile north of Lake Rebecca, in a cirque, just east of LaBohn Gap, at the foot of massive 7500′ Mt. Hinman. Like Rebecca, Rowena has plentiful numbers of small, successfully reproducing cutthroat.

Spade Lake
(5050) (122 acres)
About 1 mile along the north side of Waptus Lake, tr.1337 heads straight up, crossing the Pacific Crest Trail in a grueling mile, and in three more maddening up/-down/up miles, reaches Spade Lake. This large open lake in beautiful country has long been known for good cutthroat fishing and has good spawning habitat in its outlet. Most fish are 7-10″. The small lake next to the trail just before reaching Spade has also held fish from time to time.

Venus Lake (5600) (55 acres)
Work along the east side of Spade Lake, then rough it uphill .75 mile, 700′, beginning just east of a waterfall to get to this high, rockbound lake located in lunar type country on the southwest slopes of Mt. Daniel. Venus has a self-sustaining cutthroat population which at times produces fat 16-18″ cutthroat, though most are 6-9″. Potholes in the outlet stream also hold trout. Catch and release is a good practice here.

Deadhead Lake (5300) (11 acres)
The Spade Lake trail follows the outlet from this lake about 2 miles. At around 5200′ take off uphill in the direction of the stream and follow it to the lake, another mile,

moving eastward toward the outlet stream and eventually alongside it to the lake. It is periodically stocked with rainbow or golden trout.

Upper Cle Elum River

Rd. 4330 extends 10 miles above Salmon La Sac Campground to its end above Tucquala Lake, also known as Fish Lake. Just above Salmon La Sac there is good access to the river where the Davis Peak trail crosses it. The river is heavily fished here but few anglers are willing to work their way upstream, where there are plenty of pools and riffles. The river has a fair number of small rainbow and a few cutthroat but there are enough 10" and better in secluded spots to make for a nice day's fishing, although at times the trout are very uncooperative.

The road travels above the river for a distance and there are inviting views down into the canyon but for the most part it is risky getting in until the road drops closer to the river in about 3 miles. The next approximately 1 mile of river is bordered by private property but there is plenty of fishable water above that. Below Tucquala Lake the river becomes a meandering meadow stream for a time before it picks up speed. There are some tributaries which hold brookies and cutthroat, notably Fortune Creek. Just above the lake, the stream picks up speed again and from here on up, it holds mostly small eastern brook, eager to take a dry fly. If you can find easy to reach pools along this part of the river, it is a good place to introduce kids to stream fishing. Keeping a few for the frying pan won't hurt the brookie stock.

Tucquala Lake (3325) (63 acres)

Rd. 4330 above Salmon La Sac follows the Cle Elum River for several miles and parallels this lake on its east side. This popular slough-like lake on the upper Cle Elum River has brookies and a few rainbow. A boat or float tube along with a stealthy approach are most helpful. Early in the summer, there are spectacular fields of flowers along the lake and until the bordering meadow dries out, waders are necessary to get to much of the lake. Bring your mosquito repellent. To the northwest looms Cathedral Rock.

Squaw Lake (4400) (12 acres)

The Cathedral Rock trail begins at the Tucquala Meadows trailhead, located near the end of rd. 4330. It climbs 1400' in 2.3 miles to the lake, set in fine scenery on Cathedral Ridge. The lake is regularly stocked with rainbow.

Deep Lake (4450) (52 acres)

Continue beyond Squaw Lake 2 miles to the Pacific Crest Trail. Follow it downhill over 1000' and 2.9 miles to the lake, set at the foot of towering peaks. It has a naturalized self-sustaining cutthroat population, along with a few rainbow.

Circle Lake (6014) (49 acres)

Infrequently visited, this sizable lake is situated well over a mile west/northwest up a very steep grade along its outlet stream, which flows into Deep Lake. The

Tuck Lake

best access is said to be from Venus Lake. Reproducing cutthroat are abundant, most 8-12".

Deer Lakes (4600)

Two small lakes are found by hiking .5 mile south of Deep Lake on the Pacific Crest Trail, then .2 mile on the trail to Lake Vicente. The largest lake is periodically planted with rainbow but the smaller lake is too shallow to support trout.

Lake Vicente (5503) (11 acres)

Travel south of Deep Lake .5 mile on the Crest Trail, then 1.8 miles, steep at the end, to this remote lake, even though close to the PCT. Most people simply don't want to travel off the main trail to the lake. It is a beautiful glacial cirque lying in a basically treeless basin. Naturally reproducing cutthroat, mostly 6-9", inhabit this lake.

Peggy's Pond (5800) (5 acres)

The Cathedral Rock trail continues beyond Squaw Lake another 2 miles to a junction. Turn left for .3 mile, then right on a rugged trail for .7 mile to this lake, considerably larger than a pond, which along with a small tarn, lies in a fragile area on the west slope of Cathedral Rock. The lake is periodically stocked with rainbow and anglers will find fair to good fishing for 8-10" rainbow, some larger, depending upon stocking cycles.

Hyas Lake (3500) (124 acres)

A popular, nearly level 1.5 mile hike above Tucquala Lake in the headwaters of the Cle Elum River, Hyas and Little Hyas offer good brook trout angling from July through September. Fish are 8 to 14 inches, but sometimes difficult to catch. If you are willing to haul in a float tube or raft, it will improve your odds considerably.

Sprite Lake (6050) (5 acres)

A 3 mile, nearly 900′ per mile hike is what it takes to get to Sprite from the trailhead taking off from the road .7 mile above Fish Lake Guard Station. Once you reach Paddy-Go-Easy Pass, the lake is a very short distance beyond in truly spectacular country. The trail can be difficult to follow as it heads straight up to Paddy-Go-Easy Pass. Once planted with cutthroat, Sprite is occasionally stocked with rainbow.

Carrie Lake (5100) (15 acres)

About 2 miles downhill east past Paddy-Go-Easy Pass and Sprite Lake, the trail intersects with tr. 1559. Turn left and in about 1 mile, cross the outlet stream from Carrie. From here it is cross-country uphill .5 mile and 800′ gain. It was stocked with rainbow in 1981 but there is no record since.

M M Lake (5000) (3 acres)

On tr. 1595 about .5 mile beyond the outlet stream from Carrie Lake, pass M M's outlet stream. Follow it uphill .5 mile as it curves north to the lake. It is occasionally stocked with rainbow.

French Potholes (5375)& (5875) (5 acres and 6 acres)

About one mile or so beyond M M Lake's outlet, cross the outlet from these lakes. Though easy at first, access may be blocked as the outlet stream cuts through what looks like a waterfall in a steep cliff. Another route may work better. The Potholes receive periodic plants of rainbow or golden trout.

Klonaqua Lakes (5090) and (5187) (66 acres and 67 acres)

The Klonaquas receive periodic plants of rainbow. They can be reached by trail from the Paddy Go Easy trail or from the Icicle Creek Rd. The distance via Paddy Go Easy Pass is 10.8 miles, 8.8 miles from Icicle Creek. The trail passes **Bob Lake aka Little Klonaqua** (5450) (7 acres) about .5 mile before reaching lower Klonaqua. It is also periodically stocked with rainbow.

Tuck Lake (5250) (16 acres)

From the Hyas Lake trailhead, hike an easy 4.5 miles, a bit steep at the end, to a trail junction, with the trail to the right leading uphill about 900′ in 1.5 miles to Tuck, 6 miles in all. It can get crowded at this beautiful lake. It contains naturally reproducing cutthroat. Tuck's Pot lies just below.

Robin Lakes (6150) (11 and 34 acres)

Continue past Tuck Lake, crossing the outlet and climbing to the ridge, following cairns where possible, then along the ridge and upward some more, reaching Lower Robin in one glorious mile, 7.5 from the trailhead. Upper Robin's outlet flows into the lower lake and it is easily reached by a short walk. These lakes are becoming increasingly popular and great care should be exercised while fishing here. Both are periodically stocked with rainbow.

Granite Mt. Potholes (6400)

Cross-country to the west from Upper Robin Lake there are three small lakes, remote and infrequently visited. They are stocked with rainbow and provide good fishing.

Trico lake (5600)

By continuing on the Hyas Lake trail beyond the side trail to Tuck and Robin Lakes another .5 mile until it intersects with the Crest Trail at Deception Pass, then a short .3 mile on the Crest trail north, the outlet creek of Trico Lake crosses the trail and the lake lies uphill 1500'. The lake is rarely visited and it is unknown whether it holds trout.

Marmot Lake (4900) (135 acres)

Turn off the Crest Trail at Deception Pass past Hyas Lake. Take the signed trail 3.4 miles to a junction, the trail to the left leading .7 mile to Marmot, elevation gain 2300', a total of 9 miles from the trailhead, too long for most day hikers. Marmot holds good numbers of cutthroat trout. Cross-country south up Marmot's inlet stream .7 mile just beyond the tarn feeding the inlet stream lies **No Name Lake** (5600) which drains to **Jade Lake** (5400) (28 acres). It is unknown whether either lake contains trout. About .6 mile farther beyond the junction to Marmot lies **Lake Clarice** (4500) (41 acres) an eastern brook lake.

Teanaway   (Map 14)

The mainstem Teanaway River is formed by the West, Middle and North forks, which join about 7 miles up the Teanaway Rd. The mainstem joins the Yakima River just east of Cle Elum. The entire Teanaway system is slowly making a comeback from its years as a put-and-take fishery. The mainstem and North Fork are now no-bait/single barbless hook fisheries and anglers are beginning to notice improvement in the size and numbers of trout. There are rainbow, west slope cutthroat, cuttbows and whitefish, with predominately cutthroat in the upper reaches. Anglers may also encounter bull trout, steelhead and chinook, all of which must be released. The forks all clear relatively early and are frequently fishable by mid-June, subject to variations in snow-pack and rainy periods.

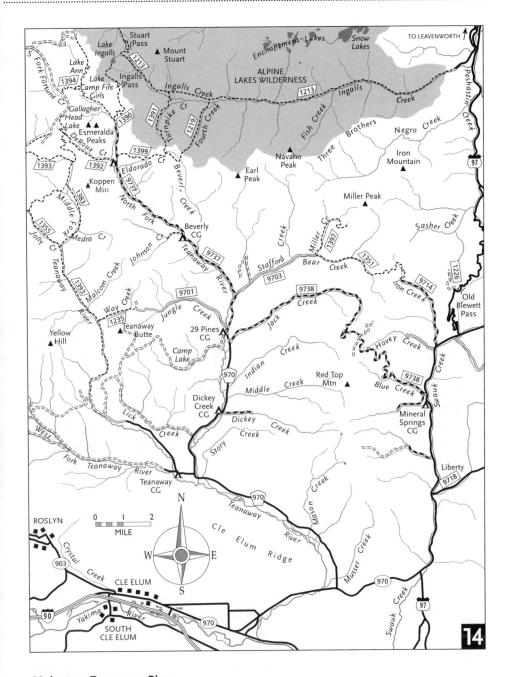

Mainstem Teanaway River.

The mainstem has fair fishing for rainbow and cutthroat from July through September, except during periods of heavy runoff. The lower section can get too low in late summer and fall to support many trout. It is accessible in only a few places below the junction of the forks, as it flows through almost entirely private property. The mainstem is a fairly large river and may well hold some big trout. Fish migrate up and down the mainstem seasonally and some experienced anglers who know where and when to fish it report fair fly fishing at times.

North Fork Teanaway River

The North Fork has the largest flow of the three forks. A road, then a trail parallel it for many miles. Those willing to walk from the end of the road may find good fishing not far up the trail in Esmeralda Basin, where, the river flattens out and there are more pools. This fork receives most of the fishing pressure on the Teanaway but the end to stocking and bait fishing has allowed the trout population to begin to reestablish itself at natural levels and fishing has improved. Holding water tends to be scarce in some reaches and a good deal of walking can be necessary to locate the best sections to fish. It is shallow for the most part and dry fly fishing is the most enjoyable and successful way to fish the North Fork.

West Fork Teanaway River

Approximately 3 miles of road parallels the West Fork and it is accessible here and there, although there is plenty of private land barring access. The West Fork is smaller than the Middle or North Fork and has lots of small cutthroat and rainbow. From the road end, a trail follows this fork for several miles. This is a good stream to introduce children to trout fishing.

Middle Fork Teanaway

A good road allows access to most of about 5 miles of the middle fork, then a trail follows it for many miles. Above the road end, there is good fishing for primarily rainbow, averaging 7-10" with a scattering of fish to 12." Few people are willing to walk even .5 mile for this kind of fishing, but those who do have fast fishing when the river is in shape. The trail, such as it is, crosses the river repeatedly. Down river from the road end, the river is fished hard where pools can be found, but still puts out fair numbers of decent trout. The middle fork clears before the north fork and is a good bet as early as the first week of June.

Gallagher Head Lake (5595) (1.5 acres)

About 2 miles prior to the end of the 23 mile North Fork Rd., which becomes rd. 9737 at 29 Pines Campground, a short spur road leads to a trailhead at De Roux Campground You can hike from here 4 miles to intersect a 4 wheel drive trail that shortly passes by this small lake. 4WDs can drive right up to the shore. This high alpine lake in open meadowland at the foot of rugged peaks was not long ago only accessible by trail. It was historically planted with rainbow and cutthroat but stocking has not occurred for some time.

Lake Ingalls (6463) (17 acres)

From the end of the North Fork Rd., an elevation of 4200', hike .4 mile to a junction, keeping right, then 2 steep miles to 5600' and another junction, finally left on the trail to Ingalls, a total of 3 miles, a 2200' gain. Carry water, as this is a dry hike. The lake is treeless, has a unique blue color, and good views of Mt. Stuart. It is a small bit of heaven in danger of overuse. It is regularly stocked with rainbow.

Upper Ingalls Creek

Ingalls creek is closed to fishing from its mouth to the Wilderness Boundary, about .5 mile up the Ingalls Creek trail, which heads up off of Highway 97. Above this point, the river is boulder and plunge pool for about 2 miles, until it flattens out. In this seldom fished section, the creek is rather sizable and provides nice wilderness fishing for trout to 12."

Lake Ann (6156) (3 acres)

Instead of taking the right fork .4 mile in on the trail to Lake Ingalls, take the left one, winding 2.7 miles to nearly 6000,' then turn right and in slightly over a mile, reach this small lake. 4WD's can get within about 1.5 miles of the lake from the upper end of this trail at Van Epps Pass, so you're likely to have company. It has been historically stocked but may not presently contain trout.

Middle Fork Teanaway River

Yakima River near Thorp

Yakima River

The Yakima River from Lake Easton to the Roza Dam outside Yakima has long been the best place in Washington to fish for large wild trout. For many years the regulations have allowed only catch and release fishing and there has been no stocking. Gradually, the size of the average trout has increased to perhaps 12" with many trout in the 15-18" range and a few giants as large as 27." An occasional steelhead may be among the largest.

Recently a salmon hatchery has been built near Cle Elum and releases large numbers of immature salmon, hoping for a substantial return. The combination of hatchery chinook with wild chinook may bring an exciting salmon fishery in the Yakima but some anglers are worried about the effect upon the wild trout population. Time will tell whether these hatchery salmon have any effect on the resident trout population but biologists are optimistic, since wild Chinook and wild trout have historically co-existed in the river. Yakima regulars reported a substantial increase in anadromous fry and smolts once the hatchery became operational but had not seen a decrease in size in resident trout after the first two years of hatchery fish in the river.

The river is open all year above Roza Dam with selective, catch and release fishing regulations but one seldom sees spin fishermen, who can do very well in the Yakima, often outfishing fly anglers when there is no hatch. March, April and May have beautiful, sunny days along with stormy, windy and cold weather. There are good hatches during these months, primarily Blue Wing Olive, March Brown, small yellow Stoneflies, and Caddis, especially toward Mother's Day. The river can be blown out by storms and it is always best to check ahead for current conditions, but it is generally low and clear until the irrigation releases from the reservoirs feeding the river begin in May. Occasionally, after storms or during heavy snow melt, the Teanaway River can discolor the Yakima for several days all the way to the Roza Dam.

Once the irrigation releases begin, until they are usually terminated in early September, the river rises, falls, rises, falls and is often very high for much of the summer. During this time, the fish feed sporadically and irregularly, with the result that even veteran anglers are skunked. Two general rules apply during this time: don't bother fishing unless there is at least a foot or more of visibility; fish the banks, where the water clears more readily and fish like to hang out in high water. With the advent of the Internet, anglers can get almost daily reports from the Yakima from various web sites. These reports are reliable and very helpful, especially during the summer irrigation season.

Yakima river trout generally feed more heavily late in the afternoon and it is not regarded as a good fishing river in the morning with occasional exceptions. Springtime, however, brings mid-day hatches.There are often short, furious feeding periods just before dark in warm weather. One can fish all day without seeing a fish rise, only to see hundreds at dusk.

The river from Ellensburg downstream to the Roza Dam, the "canyon" to most locals, is the most dependable for hatches and rising large fish. Fish rise in some canyon stretches nearly every day of the year, even if only periodically or for a few minutes. In some of these reaches, patient anglers will find large trout rising perhaps only once every 10 to 15 minutes in the same lie, allowing for some really challenging pinpoint flyfishing.

It is often very windy on the Yakima and a heavy wind makes fishing uncomfortable, difficult and in particular, makes dry fly fishing nearly impossible unless

Yakima River Rainbow Trout

fish are actively feeding. A moderate wind will not prevent decent dry fly fishing. Whether there will be wind on any given day is virtually unpredictable so one has to be ready to deal with it.

Floating is the best way to fish the Yakima, but it is relatively easy to wade. Yakima River veterans have their favorite wading areas, particularly those where there are side channels with clearer water and shallower riffles during high water, as well as spots where one can work along a bank upstream to rising fish.

Once the river settles down, clears and stabilizes after the irrigation season ends, anglers fish it much as they would any sizable river, reaching holding lies with relative ease. Fall fishing can be great on the Yakima, using all typical fall flies into October. The river supports some October Caddis, which work well for a few weeks. As temperatures drop, small mayflies such as Mahogany Duns and Blue Wing Olives attract trout. Anglers use streamers successfully before and after hatches. Eventually, about all that hatches by Thanksgiving are midges, which hatch throughout Winter into Spring, but often for only an hour or so a day. November through March finds anglers using nymphs and streamers, looking for the midge hatch if they can find it.

Downstream from Roza Dam there continues to be good fishing for sizable trout, but the season here is not open year around. As the river heads down through the city of Yakima there are some reaches with good trout fishing but a lot of searching is necessary and access is limited. Downstream, mostly below Prosser to its mouth, there is excellent flyfishing and spin fishing for smallmouth in places known to local anglers.

Appendix
Catch and Release

Catch and release has become a very important part of trout fishing in Washington. Fly anglers have embraced the practice to the point that they seldom keep trout and spin anglers are increasingly adopting catch and release as well. Throughout this book, catch and release is emphasized as a practice which is necessary to allow self-sustaining trout populations, and in turn, good fishing, to continue and improve.

Releasing a Trout

It is recommended that anglers always use single barbless hooks. Barbless hooks minimize damage to fish and facilitate successful release. Hold the fish gently, avoid touching the gills or gill covers. Leave the fish in the water while removing the hook. Very small needlenose pliers or hemostats are helpful. If the hook cannot be easily removed, cut the leader. The hook will eventually dissolve. If the fish is lethargic or exhausted after the hook is removed, hold it in a swimming position in the water and move it back and forth gently, until you release it.

Using the No Trace Ethic

Historically, the Forest Service and private timber companies such as Weyerhauser have been concerned by angler use of the forests, particularly high mountain lakes, which are very fragile. At times, anglers have been singled out, with some justification, as users who care more about fishing than taking care of the forest environment, leaving fishing line, messy campsites, garbage, fish entrails and generally disturbing riparian enviroments. Access has been restricted in some cases due to environmental abuse and there has been little support for enhancing fishing opportunities where there has been such abuse.

The surest way to reduce angler opportunity in forest lands is to leave indelible signs of camping and fishing. While anglers may have exercised poor judgment in the past to some extent, they increasingly now use the no-trace ethic in the Central Cascades. It is important that all anglers use this ethic, not only because it is the right thing to do, but also because it is pragmatically in their best interest as well.

The fundamental practices of the no-trace ethic are:

Group Size: Limit your group size while hiking and camping, as smaller groups have less impact on the land.

Travel: Do not shortcut established trail switchbacks. Staying on the trail prevents erosion. When traveling off established trails, watch where you step, especially above timberline where plant life is fragile and easily destroyed.

Finding a Campsite: Choose an area which will allow you to leave it without any trace of your use. Locate an area which does not require any leveling; in a wooded area on bare ground or forest litter at least 200 feet away from any lakes and streams;

away from trails and main areas of attraction; with serveral available routes to and from camp to minimize damage to soils and plants.

Campfires: In many forest areas, campfires are not allowed. It is far preferable to carry a portable stove. If campfires are allowed, never cut live or standing dead trees. Always use existing fire-rings if available; otherwise, clear the ground to soil. Do not line with rocks and keep away from logs, roots, brush and tree trunks. Keep the fire small. When the fire is not needed, drown and stir it, with a stick or trowel. Be sure the fire is dead out, then bury the ashes and return the area to its natural state before leaving.

Sanitation: Dig a small hole 6 inches deep and at least 200 feet from the water, trails or campsites, bury human waste and toilet paper, replace the soil, and restore the site as nearly as possible. Carry water to the campsite for washing and bathing. Avoid using soap, using biodegradable soap when necessary. Dispose of waste water well away from lakes and streams.

Leave No Trace: Pack out everything you carry in. Place all trash in a litter bag, including plastic, cans, tinfoil, and leftover food items. Don't burn or bury any of these items. Carry out every kind of litter, including anything left by others. Restore the area to its natural state.

USFS Regulations and Alpine Lakes Wilderness Regulations

There are general regulations applicable to all Wilderness areas managed by the Forest Service and additional specific regulations governing the Alpine Lakes Wilderness. It is not possible in this book to state what permits or fees will be required presently or in the future with any certainty. For current regulations, contact the nearest USFS District Ranger Office at one of the locations listed below.

Useful Information

Ranger Stations: For current information on roads and trails, and occasionally on fishing, Rangers are the angler's best source.

North Bend Ranger Station:	(425) 888-1421
Snoqualmie Pass Visitor Information Center:	(425) 434-6111
Cle Elum Ranger Station:	(509) 674-4411

Tackle and Fly Fishing Shops

Local tackle and fly fishing stores are very helpful in providing current fishing information.

Avid Angler 11714 15th NE Seattle, Wa.	206-362-4030
Creekside Angling Co. 1660 NW Gilman Blvd. #C-5, Issaquah, Wa.	425-392-3800
Kauffman's Streamborn 15015 Main, Bellevue, Wa.	425-643-2246
1918 Fourth Ave, Seattle, Wa.	206-448-0601
Linc's Fishing Tackle 501 Rainier Ave So., Seattle, Wa.	206-324-7600
Mad Flyfisher 2020 S. 320th Suite N. Federal Way, Wa.	253-945-7414
Orvis 911 Bellevue Way NE, Bellevue, Wa.	425-452-9138
Outdoor Emporium 420 Pontius N. Seattle, Wa.	206-624-6550
Patrick's Flyshop 2237 Eastlake E. Seattle, Wa.	206-325-8988
Shoff's Tackle Supply 214 W. Meeker Kent, Wa.	253-852-4760
Sportco 4602 20th St E. Fife, Wa	253-922-2222
Swede's Fly Shop 17419 139th Ave NE Woodinville, Wa.	425-487-3747
Ted's Sport Center 15526 Hwy 99 Lynwood, Wa.	425-743-9505
Xstream FlyFishing 2922 S. 112th Tukwila, Wa.	206-762-6170

Topographic Maps and Guidebooks

Green Trails maps are the best topo maps of the area. PO Box 1272, Bellevue, Wa. Ranger Offices also have topo maps, some of which have more current road information than Green Trails maps. There are several hiking guidebooks available published by the Mountaineers, 1001 SW Klickitat Way Suite 201, Seattle, WA 98134, 206-223-6303.

Sources

Washington State Game Deparment High Lake Survey 1975 King & Pierce Counties

Washington State Game Department Fishery Managment Reporty 85-3 Cutthroat in the Fuller Mountain Lakes – a Wild Trout Management Proposal

1996 Wenatchee National Forest Stream Surveys   USFS

High Lakes Fifth Field Watersheds survey – Description of Location, Surface Area, Elevation, Historically Planted and Present Fish Species, and Current Stocking and Reproductive Success   USFS

Washington State Fishing Guide, Seventh Edition, Stan Jones Publications

Lakes of Washington, Ernest Wolcott

Unpublished High Lake surveys, WDFW

Unpublished Stream Reports, WDFW

King County Mountain Lakes, Kent Hansen 1962

Snohomish County Mountain Lakes, Kent Hansen 1964

Kittitas County Mountain Lakes, Kent Hansen 1965

Index to Lakes, Rivers and Streams

About the Author

Dave Shorett was born and raised in Seattle. He has been fishing the Northwest for 45 years. Spending summers hiking and fishing the area, he is intimately familiar with the lakes and streams in the Central Cascades and brings a wealth of experience and knowledge to the subject.   He is the author of the Olympic Mountains Fishing Guide and the Mt. Rainier and South Cascades Fishing Guide.